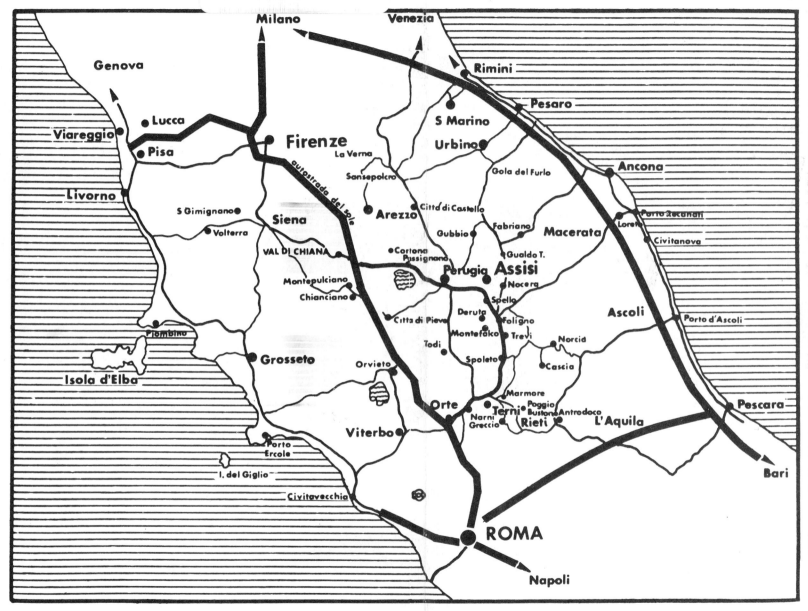

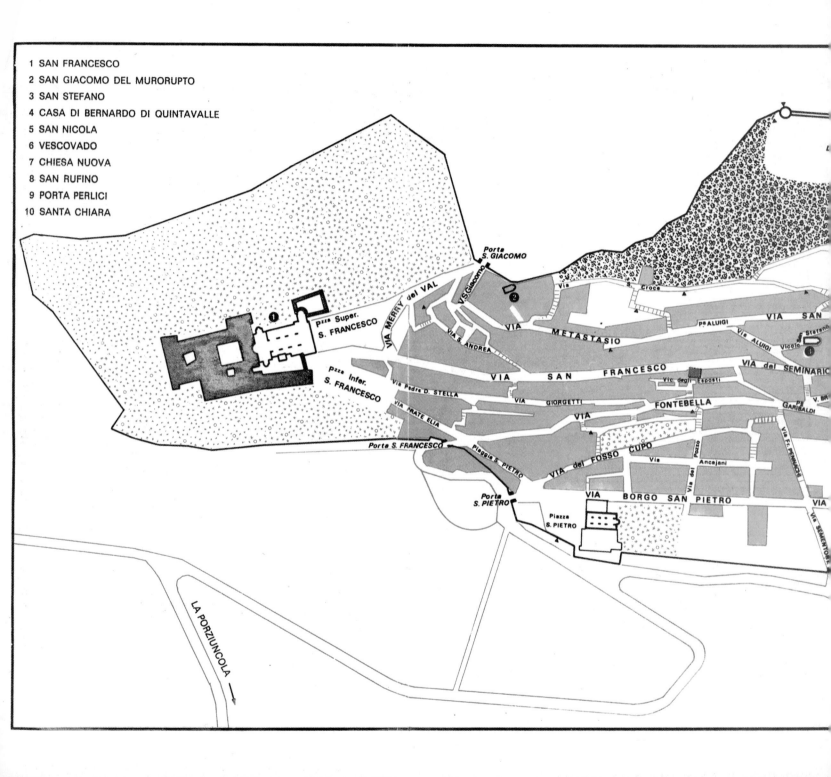

1 SAN FRANCESCO
2 SAN GIACOMO DEL MURORUPTO
3 SAN STEFANO
4 CASA DI BERNARDO DI QUINTAVALLE
5 SAN NICOLA
6 VESCOVADO
7 CHIESA NUOVA
8 SAN RUFINO
9 PORTA PERLICI
10 SANTA CHIARA

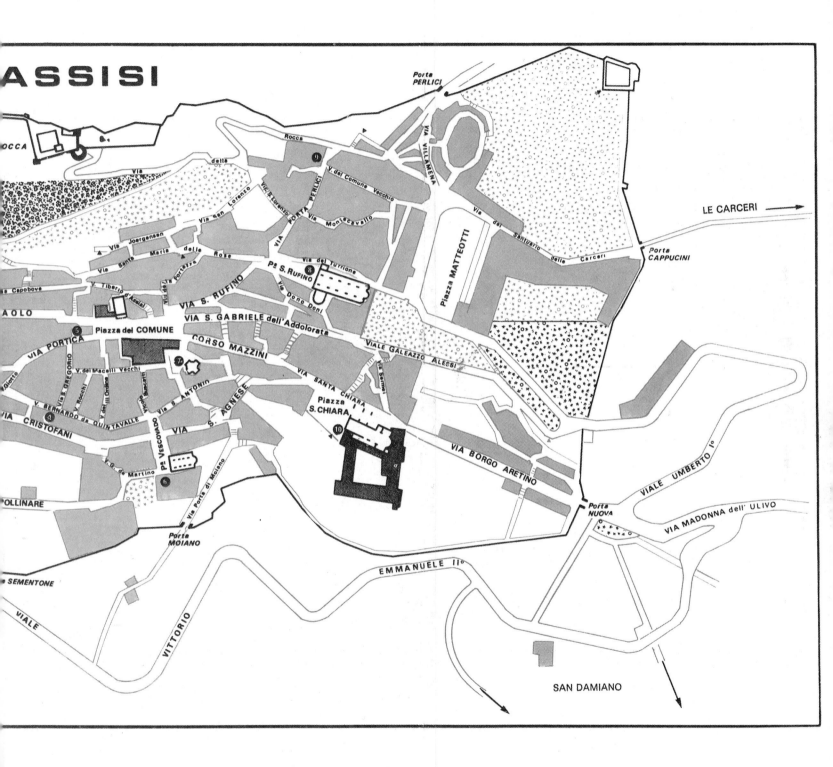

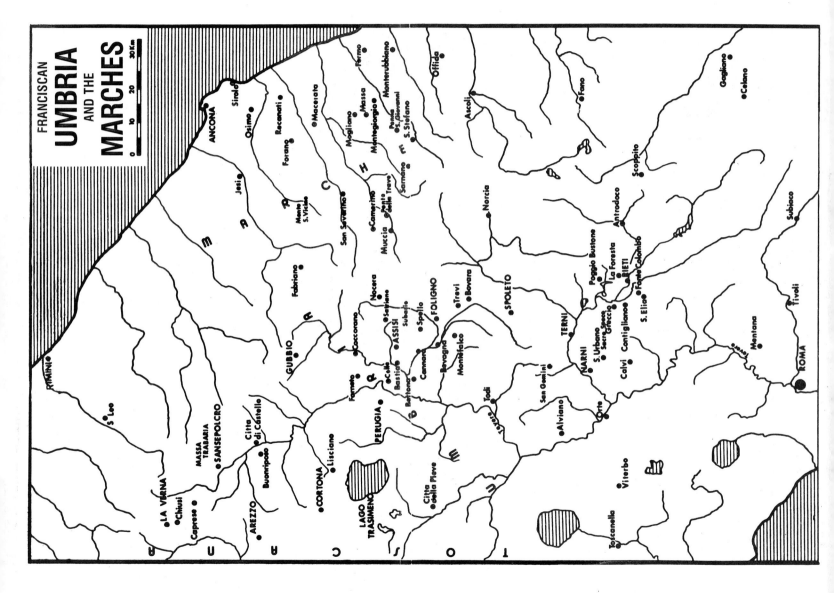

FRANCISCAN
UMBRIA
AND THE
MARCHES

0   10   20   30 Km

P. Théophile DESBONNETS

ASSISI

in the Footsteps of St. Francis

a spiritual guidebook

Original Title:

Assise sur les pas de saint François
Ed. Franciscaines, Paris, 1971

Translated from the French by:
Sr. Nancy Celaschi, O.S.F.

Second edition

© Edizioni Porziuncola 1993
   Via Protomartiri Francescani
   S. Maria degli Angeli - Assisi (PG)

ASSISI

More than an important center of art, Assisi is the city where St. Francis gave birth to a new spirit. The freshness of that spirit is still capable of attracting us to a simplicity, joy, and peace which are hard to find. This book is for those readers, whether pilgrims or tourists, who want to discover that source.

Therefore, the important thing about Assisi is not Giotto, but St. Francis. He wanted to follow Christ; that is what all of the saints want to do. Although no one has ever totally succeeded, each one had his or her own style; Francis' is totally unique!

In order to understand the Franciscan spirit, the mystery of Assisi, it is best to simply immerse yourself in the atmosphere of the region where Francis walked, the city where he was born and spent his entire life.

Take your time! Don't hurry from this Giotto to that Lorenzetti, nor even from one sanctuary to the next. Forget about those detailed guide-books to Assisi; investigate the alleys and pathways where the pink and white rocks call out to you from the walls of an ancient house. Climb a stairway where the sun provides a pocket of light as an invitation to peace and joy. Don't worry about getting lost; you may only end up walking a little extra!

At almost every step you will encounter St. Francis; this book is merely an attempt to help you meet him "in truth". Or that, we think the best guide is Francis himself, or at least his first followers. They were eyewitnesses, and it is to them that we look to nourish our reflection on this visit to Assisi.

Bibliography

There is no lack of books about St. Francis of Assisi; bookstores abound with them. They are also available through public libraries in collections of literature, biography, and fiction.

The sources used in this work can be found in the following texts:

Francis and Clare, The Complete Works. Regis Armstrong, O.F.M. Cap. and Ignatius Brady, O.F.M., trans. Paulist Press, 1982.

St. Francis of Assisi, Omnibus of Sources. Marion Habig, ed. Franciscan Herald Press, 1973.

St. Clare of Assisi, Nesta De Robeck. Franciscan Herald Press, 1980.

Clare of Assisi, Early Documents. Edited and translated by Regis J. Armstrong, O.F.M. Cap., Paulist Press, 1988.

Legends, Not Myths

Throughout this book many "legends" are cited as source material. The word legend is a technical term meaning something written to be read, usually as spiritual reading or "Lectio Divina", as it was known in Latin. The reader should not think that these are make-believe fairy tales, but are probably grounded in historical fact.

How to use this guide

A quick glance at the Table of Contents (p 139) will reveal the organization of this book. You will find.:

A **Bibliography** (p. 4) and a **Chronology** of the life of St. Francis (p. 11); this will help you remember the main events in the life of St. Francis.

Several **Pratical Hints** (p. 6) to help you plan your trip to Assisi and find your way around the city.

Several **Itineraries** (p. 9) for those who want a detailed plan.

One large map of Assisi and several smaller ones to help you find your way.

The **Notes** on the various places. Since the best way to visit Assisi is to do it without a pre-planned itinerary, these notes are arranged alpabetically. From page 15 to page 115 you will find: the Carceri, Casa Gualdi, Chiesa Nuova, the House of Bernardo da Quintavalle, the Porta Perlici, the Porziuncola, Rivotorto, the Rocca, San Damiano, San Francesco, San Nicolò, San Rufino, Santa Chiara, the Streets of Assisi and the Vescovado.

Each note consists of a selection of texts and a guide; the texts are the accounts from the Franciscan sources about the place under consideration. These texts should help the reader discover the Franciscan spirit. Generally, we would advise your reading them before visiting the place.

Although this book is not meant to be a complete guide, each section indicates a few things which you will not want to overlook.

The last section indicates some excursions outside the city which can enhance our journey "in the footsteps of St. Francis".

Practical hints

1. Travelling to Assisi

By Car

You will almost necessarily find yourself travelling Rte. A 1, the "Autostrada del Sole".

From the North (Florence-Assisi = 185 km.) Exit at Val di Chiana; follow the signs for **Perugia**, passing by **Cortona**, which is directly on the highway.

Or, you can exit at **Chiusi-Chianciano**. In either case, you will drive along the shores of **Lake Trasimeno**, noted for Hannibal's victory in 277 B.C.; it also reminds us of the Lent which Francis spent on the Isola Maggiore (*Fioretti 7*).

From the South (Rome-Assisi = 170 km.). Exit at **Orte**, follow S.S. 3 (Via Flaminia) for **Terni, Spoleto** and **Foligno**. Take S.S. 75 the rest of the way. Those who have the time to spare should consider leaving S.S. 3 at **Terni,** continuing on to the **Rieti Valley,** and visiting the Franciscan hermitages of **Greccio, Fonte Colombo, La Foresta** and **Poggio Bustone**. Continue to **Assisi.** You can go from **Rome** to **Rieti** directly by way of S.S. 4 (Via Salaria).

By Train

The train station, **Sta. Maria degli Angeli,** 4 km. outside of Assisi, is located on the **Foligno-Terontola** line. It is served by trains to both **Rome** and **Florence;** you will have to change trains in either **Foligno** or **Terontola**. There is regular bus service to **Assisi** from the train station.

2. Parking

It is extremely difficult to go through **Assisi** by car; it's even harder to find a parking place. Anyways, it is advisable to go through **Assisi** on foot; that's the best way to discover its charm.

Parking areas are located at **Porta S. Pietro,** below **Porta Nuova**, at **Piazza Matteotti** and the **Piazza Inferiore** of **S. Francesco**.

3. Camping

Campers will find an excellent campsite (Camping **Fontemaggio**) on the road to the **Carceri.**

4. To San Damiano

San Damiano is located about 800 m. outside of the **Porta Nuova**. To go there on foot, pass trough the **Porta Nuova** and take the first path on the right. This will skirt a large parking lot, pass under the **Viale Vittorio Emanuele** and lead to **San Damiano.**

The route described above is not accessible by car. Go through the **Porta Nuova;** take the **Viale Vittorio Emmanuele** and take the first road on the left.

5. To the Carceri

The Carceri is situated about 4 km. from Assisi; the road to the Carceri leaves Assisi at the **Porta dei Cappuccini.**

To go by car, leave the city at the **Porta Nuova,** take the **Viale Umberto I** (to the left when leaving the city.) This road doubles back and re-enters the city at **Piazza Matteotti.** Again doubling back, you will find **Via delle Carceri,** which leaves the city through the **Porta dei Cappuccini.** Toward the end of the road there is a narrow section. Parking is located near the entrance to the hermitage, but, once inside, there is still about 100 meters to climb.

When going on foot, leave **Piazza del Comune,** take **Via S. Rufino** then, at the left of the cathedral, **Via del Turrione.** This will take you to the **Piazza Matteotti;** continue as above.

6. To the Rocca

To reach the **Rocca** by car, begin with the directions given for the Carceri i.e, **Porta Nuova**, **Viale Umberto I, Piazza Matteotti.** At the end of the Piazza, take **Via Villamena** (on the left) toward the **Porta Perlici.** A sharp left-hand turn leads to the **Via della Rocca** which is very narrow in places.

To go there by foot, you have several choices; the easiest is from the **Piazza del Comune, Via. S. Rufino, Via Porta Perlici** and, on the left, **Vicolo S. Lorenzo.**

7. Visiting the sanctuaries

In most of the sanctuaries you can probably ask for a guided tour by a Franciscan. If interested, inquire at the **Sacristy** or at the entrance.

Index of names

Itineraries

The best way to discover Assisi is by following the inspiration of the moment. However, for those who prefer more definite plans, we offer several itineraries, based on the amount of time available. A visit to the **Porziuncola** can be added on to any of these; that, as well as a visit to **San Damiano** cannot be neglected.

1. A half day

Park at **Porta San Pietro**. Take **Via Frate Elia** to **San Francesco**. After visiting the Basilica, take **Via S. Francesco** toward the center of the city. (A possible variation: take **Via Merry del Val** toward **Porta San Giacomo**, and take the picturesque **Vicolo Sant'Andrea** to rejoin **Via S. Francesco**.) On this side of the **Piazza del Comune** there are the remains of **San Nicolo**. Continue on to the Cathedral of **San Rufino**, exit by the side door and go down to **Santa Chiara**. From there, go directly to **San Damiano**. (Or, by way of **Via Sant'Agnese, Santa Maria Maggiore**, the **Vescovado** and the **Church of San Pietro**, return to **Porta San Pietro** and go by car to **San Damiano**).

2. A whole day

Park at **Porta San Pietro**. Go directly to **Chiesa Nuova** (near the **Piazza del Comune**.) To do so, take **Via Fontebella, Via Brizzi, Via Giotto** and **Via Portica**. From there, go up to **San Rufino**, exit through the side door and go down to **Santa Chiara**. By way of **Via Sant'Agnese**, go to the **Vescovado**; continue on to the house of **Bernardo di Quintavalle**. Return to the **Piazza del Comune** by way of **Via S. Gregorio** and visit the remains of **San Nicolo**. Leave the Piazza by way of **Via S. Paolo**; take **Via S. Stefano** (on the left) and visit the little church of **Santo Stefano**.

Countinuing along **Via S. Stefano,** take a left turn on **Via Aluigi, Via Arnaldo Fortini** and head toward **San Francesco** on **Via S. Francesco.** Visit the Basilica and go to the **Porta San Pietro.** By car, go to **San Damiano** and the **Carceri**.

3. Two or more days

If you have two or more days to spend in Assisi, you can afford to be less selective in choosing the sites to visit. In that case, begin with a climb to **La Rocca;** follow Itinerary 2, but make the following adjustments:

A. After visiting **San Rufino**, visit, in that area, the **Palazzo dei Consoli**, the ancient church of **Santa Maria delle Rose**, the oratory of **San Lorenzo**, the ancient **Porta Perlici** and **old Assisi.**

B. After visiting **Santa Chiara,** go to **San Damiano** by way of the **Porta Nuova.** Return to Assisi through the **Porta Moiano** (or take the country roads toward **San Masseo** where you can find the crypt integrated into the farm buildings) Re-enter Assisi by the **Porta Sementone.**

C. Before or after visiting **San Francisco,** visit **San Giacomo de Murorupto**.

D. When visiting the **Porziuncola**, proceed to **Rivo Torto.**

Chronology of the life of St. Francis

1182   **Francis is born in Assisi**; he is baptized "John", but his father, returning from a trip to France, calls him Francis.

1198   The citizens of Assisi destroy the Rocca, a symbol of the imperial presence.

1199-1200   Civil war in Assisi; the commune is established.

1202   (November) – War between Assisi and Perugia. At the battle of Ponte San Giovanni, Francis is captured and taken as a prisoner to Perugia.

1203   Francis is freed and returns to Assisi; he is ill.

1204   Francis' long illness.

1205   (spring) – Francis decides to respond to the Pope's call for a Crusade. Magnificently armed, he leaves home. At Spoleto, he is told in a dream to return home.

1205   (summer) – Grace continues to work in Francis. "King of the youth of Assisi", he has one final celebration with his friends.

1205   **At San Damiano**, Francis hears the Crucifix say to him, **"Repair my house!"**. In Foligno, Francis sells some cloth and offers the money to the priest at San Damiano; the latter refuses it. Francis' conflict with his father begins.

1206   (spring) – **Francis renounces his patrimony in front of the Bishop** and leaves for Gubbio.

1206   (summer) – Francis returns to Assisi dressed as a hermit and begins to repair San Damiano.

1206   (summer) to **1208** (February) – Francis successively repairs San Damiano, a chapel dedicated to St. Peter, and the Porziuncola.

1208   (February 24) – **At the Porziuncola**, Francis hears **the Gospel for the feast of St. Matthias**; he discovers his vocation of evangelic poverty. He modifies his garb, changing his leather belt for a rope cincture. He begins to preach.

1208   (April 16) – Bernardo di Quintavalle and Peter Catanii join Francis.

1208   (April 23) – Giles joins them.

1208   (summer) – Three new members, one of them named Philip, join the young fraternity.

1208   (late) – The second mission; seven members go to Poggio Bustone and preach throughout the Rieti Valley. A new member joins them; they go two by two on the third mission.

1209   (early) – The eight return to the Porziuncola. Four members join.

1209   (spring) – **Francis writes a short rule** and he leaves for Rome with his first eleven brothers. Pope **Innocent III approves their way of life**. On their return, they stay for a short time near Orte, then settle at Rivo Torto.

1209   or **1210** – Chased out of Rivo Torto, **the friars go to the Porziuncola**.

1211   (summer?) – Francis plans a mission to Syria; cross-winds ruin the plans.

1212   (March 18-19) – On the night after Palm Sunday, Francis **receives Clare** into the order at the Porziuncola; the order of the Poor Ladies begins. Several weeks later, Clare and her companions move to San Damiano.

1213   (May 8) – Count Roland of Chiusi offers Francis the mountain of La Verna to build a hermitage.

1215   (November) – Francis is in Rome for the Fourth Lateran Council; there he probably meets St. Dominic.

1216   (July 16) – Pope Innocent III dies in Perugia. Two days later, Honorius III is chosen to replace him. At this time, Francis probably meets Archbishop Jacques de Vitry.

1216   (summer) – In Perugia Francis obtains from Pope Honorius the **Indulgence** to commemorate the consecration **of the Porziuncola**.

1217   (May 5) – General Chapter at the Porziuncola. The first missions cross the Alps and the Mediterranean. Francis plans to go to France, but Cardinal Ugolino meets him in Florence and persuades him to stay in Italy.

1219 (end of June) – Francis leaves Ancona for Acre and Damietta.

1219 (autumn) – **Francis meets the Sultan**. Later, he visits the Holy Land.

1220 (spring and summer) – Alerted to the difficulties occurring within the Order during his absence, Francis returns to Italy with Peter Catanii, Elias and Caesar of Speyer. **He resigns as Minister General** and chooses Peter Catanii to replace him. At Francis' request, Pope Honorius designates Cardinal Ugolino as Protector of the Order.

1221 (March 10) – Peter Catanii dies. Elias is designated Vicar General.

1221 (May 30) – General Chapter – **First Rule**.

1223 At Fonte Colombo, during the early part of the year, **Francis composes the Second Rule**, which is to be discussed in the General Chapter in June; Pope Honorius III approves it on November 29.

1223 (December 24-25) – **Christmas at Greccio**.

1224 (August 15-September 29) – Francis retires to La Verna to celebrate Lent in honour of St. Michael. On September 14 or 15 **he receives the Stigmata**.

1224 (October and early November) – Francis returns to the Porziuncola, passing by Borgo San Sepolcro, Monte Casale and Città di Castello.

1224-1225 (December to February) – Riding a donkey, Francis undertakes a preaching tour through Umbria and the Marches.

1225 (March to May) – His eyesight worsens; nearly blind, at the insistence of Brother Elias, Francis spends some time at San Damiano. He undergoes treatment, but there is no improvement. In the midst of these sufferings he is assured of eternal salvation; he composes the **Canticle of the Creatures**.

1225 (June) – Francis adds a verse to the Canticle and effects a reconciliation between the Bishop and the Mayor. Receiving a letter from Cardinal Ugolino, Francis leaves San Damiano for the Rieti Valley.

1225 (early July) – Francis is welcomed to Rieti by Cardinal Ugolino and the Papal Curia; he goes to Fonte Colombo for the eye treatment which Cardinal Ugolino had recommended; the treatment is delayed until Elias arrives.

1225 (September) – Francis goes to San Fabiano near Rieti; another doctor treats him. While Francis is there, the crowds ruin the vineyard of a poor priest; Francis prays and the harvest is restored.

1226 (April) – Francis is in Siena for a new treatment.

1226 (May or June) – Francis stays at "La Cella" in Cortona where he dictates his **Testament**. He later returns to the Porziuncola.

1226 (July-August) – During the summer's heat, Francis stays at Bagnara, in the mountains near Nocera.

1226 (late August or early September) – His condition worsening, Francis is returned to Assisi, passing through Satriano. There he stays in the Bishop's palace.

1226 (September) – Sensing that his death is near, Francis insists on going back to the Porziuncola.

1226 (Saturday, October 3) – **Francis dies at the Porziuncola**; the next day, he is buried in San Giorgio.

1227 (March 19) – Francis' friend, Cardinal Ugolino, becomes Pope Gregory IX.

1228 (July 16) – Gregory IX **canonizes Francis** in Assisi.

1230 (May 25) – The body of St. Francis is transferred from San Giorgio to the new basilica constructed in his honor.

The "doors of the dead"

One of the pecularities of Assisi is the number of walled-up doors that can be observed. Several houses have more than one.

Legend has it that whenever an inhabitant of Assisi died, the family would seal over the door through which the corpse had been carried out, and a new door would be made. Thus the name "porta del morto" was given to them.

As romantic as this explanation is, it is hardly reasonable. Although this is a well-documented pagan custom, it would have hardly lasted in a Christian culture.

The real reason for these doors can be found in the state of chronic insecurity in the Middle Ages, especially in the little cities which were divided into various factions. The houses had two types of doors. On the ground level, one or more doors gained access to shops or stables which were completely separate from the rest of the house. About 1 meter above the ground there was a smaller door that served as the entrance to the upper stories. A wooden stairway with various angles and curves would lead to the family quarters; the stairway was removed at night and the inhabitants were safe from attack.

Later, in less troubled times, the houses were remodeled. In some cases, they replaced the wooden steps with stone ones and kept the higher door. (Several examples can be seen in Assisi). In other houses, they added a new interior stairway to the ground floor, and used the street level entrance. The elevated doorway, which was no longer needed, was either sealed over or made into a window.

Assisi in the time of St. Francis

The Assisi that St. Francis knew was much smaller than it is today, especially running from East to West. The remains of the old 13th century city walls can be seen; these include the Arco del Seminario (via S. Francesco), the Arco dei Pucci (Corso Mazzini), and on Via Porta Perlici and Via Sant'Apollinare.

THE CARCERI

The word "Carceri" literally means "prison"; However, here it is not used in the sense of a jail, but in the religious sense of seclusion. The best translation would be "solitary confinement".

At the time of St. Francis there was probably a little chapel, several caves in the hillside, and some huts built by the first friars. The present convent was built by St. Bernardine of Siena in the 15th Century. It is so small and secluded, however, that it really does not ruin the atmosphere of the site. In many ways, the Carceri still remains as the first friars knew it.

In contrast to the Cistercians who frequently settled in the valleys, the first Franciscans preferred the heights: the Carceri, which we are considering now, as well as Greccio, Poggio Bustone and Fonte Colombo. Climbing along the hills, we sense some of Francis' delight in nature; at the Carceri however, we must certainly recall how Francis was naturally drawn toward prayer and contemplation.

Life in hermitages

Francis himself wrote a "rule" for organizing life in hermitages like the Carceri:

> Those who wish to live religiously in hermitages should be three brothers or four at the most; two of these should be mothers and they

should have two sons or at least one. The two who are mothers should follows the life of Martha while the two sons should follow the life of Mary and they may have an enclosure in which each one may have his small cell in which he may pray and sleep.

And let them seek first of all the kingdom of God and his justice.

And in the enclosure, where they live, they should not permit any person to enter, nor should they eat there. Those brothers who are the mothers should be eager to stay far from every person; and because of the obedience to their minister they should protect their sons from everyone, so that no one can talk with them. And the sons should not talk with any person except with their mothers and with the minister and his custodian when it pleases them to visit with the blessing of the Lord God. The sons however, should sometimes assume the role of the mothers, as from time to it may seem good to them to exchange roles. They should strive to observe conscientiously and carefully all the things mentioned above.

Rule for Hermitages

Retire in solitude or preach?

Francis was so drawn to contemplation that one day he questioned whether he should devote his life to it or continue preaching. He decided to ask the advice of Clare, who was at San Damiano, and of Sylvester, who was at the Carceri.

The humble servant of Christ, St. Francis, at the beginning of his conversion, when he had already gathered many companions and received them into the Order, was placed in a great agony of doubt as to what he should do: whether to give himself only to continual prayer or to preach sometimes. He wanted very much to know which of these would please our Lord Jesus Christ most. And as the holy humility that was in him did not allow him to trust in himself or in his own prayers, he humbly turned to others in order to know God's will in this matter.

So he called Brother Masseo and said to him: "Dear Brother, go to Sister Clare and tell her on my behalf to pray devoutly to God, with one of her purer and more spiritual companions, that He may deign to show me what is best, either that I preach sometimes or that I devote myself only to prayer. And then go also to Brother Sylvester, who is staying on Mount Subasio, and tell him the same thing".

This was that Lord Sylvester who had seen a cross of gold issuing from the mouth of St. Francis which extended in length to Heaven and in width to the ends of the world. And this Brother Sylvester was so devout and holy that God immediately granted or revealed to him whatever he asked in prayer. The Holy Spirit had made him remarkably deserving of divine communications and he conversed with God many times. And therefore St. Francis was very devoted to him and had great faith in him. This holy Brother Sylvester often stayed alone in the above-mentioned place.

Brother Masseo went and did as St. Francis had ordered him, gave the message first to St. Clare and then to Brother Sylvester. When the latter received it, he immediately set himself to praying. And while praying he quickly had God's answer. And he went out at once to Brother Masseo and said "The Lord says you are to tell Brother Francis this: that God has not called him to this state only on his own account, but that he may reap a harvest of souls and that many may be saved through him".

At this Brother Masseo went back to St. Clare to know what she had received from God. And she answered that both she and her companion had had the very same answer from God as Brother Sylvester.

Brother Masseo therefore returned to St. Francis. And the Saint received him with great charity: he washed his feet and prepared a meal for him. And after he had eaten, St. Francis called Brother Masseo into the woods. And there he knelt down before Brother Masseo, and baring his head and crossing his arms, St. Francis asked him:

"What does my Lord Jesus Christ order me to do?"

Brother Masseo replied that Christ had answered both Brother Sylvester and Sister Clare and her companion and revealed that "He wants you to go about the world preaching, because God did not call you for yourself alone but also the salvation of others".

And then the hand of the Lord came over St. Francis. And as soon as he heard this answer and thereby knew the will of Christ, he got to his feet, all aflame with divine power, and said to Brother Masseo with great fervor: "So let's go in the name of the Lord!".

Fioretti, 16.

Today as in Francis' day, the Carceri is a place conducive to meditation and silence. Even if you lack the time to make a retreat or spend a day there, you should try to visit this place in a spirit of recollection.

To see the Carceri

The entrance to the hermitage leads into the little courtyard (A) perched high atop the ravine. The little church (B) leads to the ancient chapel (C) which dates back to the time of Francis. On the back wall, beneath a fresco of Mary, there is an older fresco of the crucifixion. At the left of the chapel is the tiny choir (D) where the Office is recited.

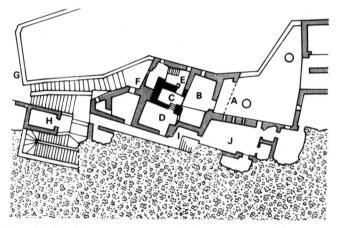

The Carceri. The oldest sections are in black.

To the right there is a narrow passage and a stairway; take this path to the Grotto of St. Francis (E). There, in a deep depression in the rock, Francis both prayed and slept. On leaving the grotto you will notice two primitive frescoes.

The Bridge (G) which crosses the ravine leads to the grotto of "Brother Leo"; going off along the various paths you will find the caves of Bernard, Sylvester, Ruffino and Masseo. However, the friars really did not have their own grottoes; anyone who stayed at the Carceri chose any available cave or hut.

Returning to the main area, visit the chapel (H) which contains the tomb of Blessed Barnabas Manassei of Terni (d. 1474), founder of the Mons Pietatis. In the old cloister you can see the large mission cross (I) of St. Bernardine of Siena. End your visit at the small refectory (J); notice the wall which is simply carved out of the hillside.

CASA GUALDI

About halfway between Assisi and Sta. Maria degli Angeli is the Casa Gualdi; it is located on the right, near an intersection. On this site in the 13th century there was a leprosarium, San Salvatore della Parete. The road running from east to west still bears the name of Via Francesca, the road of the French. This road was one of the branches of the route between France and Rome which was travelled by many pilgrims and merchants.

Kissing the leper

In the Middle Ages laws were hard on the lepers. Forced to live in leprosaria, they were forbidden to wander far from them; thus we can place Francis' encounter with the leper, one of the most important moments of his conversion, in this area.

> The Lord granted me, Brother Francis, to begin to do penance in this way: While I was in sin, it seemed very bitter to me to see lepers. And the Lord Himself led me among them and I had mercy upon them. And when I left them that which seemed bitter to me was changed into sweetness of soul and body; and afterward I lingered a little and left the world.
>
> *Testament*

> One day while Francis was praying fervently to God, he received an answer. "O Francis, if you want to know my will, you must hate and despise all that which hitherto your body has loved and desired to possess. Once you begin to do this, all that formerly seemed sweet and pleasant to you will become bitter and unbearable; and instead the things that formerly made you shudder will bring great sweetness and content". Francis was divinely comforted and greatly encouraged by these words. Then one day, as he was riding near Assisi, he met a leper. He had always felt an overpowering horror of these sufferers, but making a great effort, he conquered his aversion, dismounted, and in giving the leper a coin, kissed his hand. The leper then gave him the kiss of peace, after which Francis remounted his horse and rode on his way. From that day onwards he mortified himself increasingly until, through God's grace, he won a complete victory.

21

Some days later he took a large sum of money to the leper hospital, and gathering all the immates together, he gave them alms, kissing each of their hands. Formerly he could neither touch nor look at lepers, but when he left them on that day, what had been so repugnant to him had really and truly been turned into something pleasant. Indeed, his previous aversion to lepers had been so strong that, besides being incapable of looking at them, he would not even approach the places where they lived. And if by chance he happened to pass anywhere near their dwellings or to see one of the lepers, even though he was moved to give them an alms through some intermediate person, he would nevertheless turn his face away and hold his nose. But, strengthened by God's grace, he was enabled to obey the command and to love what he had hated and to abhor what he had hitherto wrongfully loved. In consequence of this he became such a friend to the lepers that, as he himself declared in his *Testament*, he lived with them and served them with loving eagerness.

Legend of the Three Companions, 11.

Serving the lepers

Encountering the leper played such an important role in Francis' conversion that he wanted all his brothers to have a similar experience.

From the beginning of his conversion, blessed Francis, wise that he was, decided with the help of the Lord to build not only his own life but his house, that is, his Order, called the Order of the Friars Minor, firmly on a solid rock, namely, on the most exalted humility and poverty of the Son of God.

He built it on deep humility. That is why, from the very beginning, when brothers began to multiply, he made it clear that they were to live in lazarets to serve the lepers. At that time, when postulants presented themselves, whether nobles or commoners, they were forewarned that among other things they would have to serve the lepers and live in their hospitals.

Legend of Perugia, 102.

Final blessing of Assisi

Francis wanted to die at the Porziuncola, cradle of the Order he founded. While they were carrying him there, he had the cortege stop at this intersection. He turned his face to the city of his birth and blessed it for the last time. (The plaque on the wall of the house commemorates that event).

While he was living in that palace, seeing that his sickness grew worse from day to day, he had himself carried on a stretcher to St. Mary of the Porziuncola. He could not have endured going on horseback, since it would have aggravated his very painful illness. Since those who were carrying him took the road that went past the hospital, he told them to put the stretcher on the ground so that he would be facing Assisi. For all practical purposes he could no longer see by reason of his long and serious eye-sickness. Then he raised himself a little and blessed the city of Assisi, saying:

"Lord, I believe that this city was formerly the refuge and abode of wicked and unjust men of evil repute throughout the country; but I also see that, by your superabundant goodness, at a time chosen by you, you have shown this city the riches of your love. It has become the abode and residence of those who know you as they should, who give glory to your name and diffuse the sweet fragrance of a pure life, a solid faith, and a good reputation among all Christian people. I therefore beg you, Lord Jesus Christ, Father of mercies, do not look upon our ingratitude, but recall to mind the infinite love that you have shown to this city. May it always remain the abode and residence of those who will know and glorify your blessed and glorious name in the ages to come. Amen".

CHIESA NUOVA

In this section of the city, near the Piazza del Comune, St. Francis was born and spent his childhood and youth. Two sanctuaries commemorate that period of his life: *San Francesco Picolo and Chiesa Nuova.*

San Francesco Picolo

Behind the door of this tiny oratory there is the following inscription: **"Hoc oratorium fuit bovis et asini stabulum in quo natus est sanctus Franciscus mundi speculum".** (This oratory was the stable where Francis, the mirror of the world, was born).

They say that Francis' mother came to this stable to give birth to her son. This is obviously a legend, a fruit of the development of the "Conformities of the life of Francis to the life of Christ". However, this is even a later development because in his 14th century book, Bartholoew of Pisa does not mention it.

The legendary nature of this event, as exaggerated as it may be, does remind us of a certain truth: Francis left the world to follow Christ.

We should also bear in mind that this place, known as the Oratory of St. Francis since the 13th century, is probably the best-documented site of the house of Francis.

Chiese Nuova

This church was built in the 17th century on the foundations of an old house, parts of which were incorporated into the church. According to an old tradition (Louis di Città di Castello cites it in 1570), it is supposed to be the house of Pietro di Bernardone. This rich merchant could have owned both houses, either simultaneously or successively.

Leaving the arguments to the scholars, let us consider Francis' youth.

A promising youth

The young Francis wasn't exactly a little saint; he was like the other children of his time and like the children of all times:

> Francis grew up quick and clever, and he followed in his father's footsteps by becoming a merchant. In business, however, he was very different from Peter, being far more high-spirited and open-handed. He was also intent on games and songs; and day and night he roamed about the city of Assisi with companions of his own age. He was a spend-thrift, and all that he earned went into eating and carousing with his friends. For this his parents often remonstrated with him, saying that in squandering such large sums on himself and others, his style of living made him appear not so much their son as the son of a great prince. However, being rich and loving him tenderly, they allowed him free rein in order to avoid displeasing him. When the Lady Pica heard the neighbors commenting on their son's extravagance, she answered:
>
> "What do you think my son will be? Through grace he will become a son of God".
>
> In all things Francis was lavish, and he spent much more on his clothes than was warranted by his social position. He would use only the finest materials; but sometimes his vanity took an eccentric turn, and then he would insist on the richest cloth and the commonest being sewn together in the same garment.
>
> *Legend of the Three Companions, 2.*

A surprising lack of courtesy

Francis had the reputation of being very courteous. One day, however, he brusquely sent a poor man away. Realizing what he had done, his conversion took another step forward:

> One day when he was in the shop selling cloth, a beggar came in and asked for alms for the love of God; but Francis was so intent on the business of making money that he gave nothing to the poor man. Then, enlightened by divine grace, he accused himself harshly, saying: "If that beggar had made his request in the name of some great prince, you would have surely given him what he asked; how much more so you should have done it when he begged in the name of the King of kings and Lord of all!" Taught by this experience, he resolved in his heart never again to refuse anything that might be asked of him in the name of God.
>
> *Legend of the Three Companions, 3.*

A dream

Francis had a burning desire to become a knight. However, when he was at the point of leaving to join Walter of Brienne, he had a strange dream which he did not fully understand.

> While Francis was asleep, a man appeared who called him by name and led him into a vast and pleasant palace in which the walls were hung with glittering coats of mail, shining bucklers, and all the weapons and armor of warriors. Francis was delighted, and reflecting on what could be the meaning of all this, he asked for whom the splendid arms and beautiful palace were intended; and he received the answer that they were for him and his knights.
>
> On awaking, Francis rose gleefully, thinking, after the manner of worldlings (for he had not yet tasted the spirit of God) that he was destined to become a magnificent prince and that the vision was prophetic of great prosperity.
>
> What he had seen spurred him on to start for Apulia and to get himself knighted in the following of Count Gentile. His glee was such that people, in surprise, asked the reason of his delight and received the answer: "I know that I shall become a great prince".
>
> *Legend of the Three Companions, 5.*

A touching deed

Francis began to be converted, and even his behavior at home was changed:

> Sometimes it happened that Francis remained in the house alone with his mother while his father was away on business; on these occasions he would heap the table with loaves, both for dinner and supper, as though for the whole family. One day his mother asked him why he prepared so much bread, and he replied that he wished to distribute the loaves to those in need because he had promised always to give alms to anyone who begged from him in God's name. His mother loved him more than her other children, and therefore she let him have his way in these things but she observed all he did, and often secretly marveled at it.
>
> In former years he had so enjoyed the company of his friends that he was always ready to join them; they only had to call and Francis would leave the table and be off, having barely tasted his food, and leaving his parents greatly distressed at such untimely haste. Now, however, his whole heart was entirely bent on seeing, hearing, and attending to the poor; and he gave them generous alms in the name of God.

Legend of the Three Companions, 9.

An angry father

Now Francis was really on the way to conversion. Having heard Christ speaking to him at San Damiano, he began to lead a life of penance. That wasn't exactly what his father had in mind; the following episode occurred in their family home, which Francis would soon leave for good:

> When his friends and relatives saw him, they covered him with insults, calling him a fool and a madman, and hurling stones and mud at him. Seeing him so changed, they thought he must be out of his mind.
>
> But God's servant paid no heed to all this; unmoved by insults, he thanked almighty God for everything.
>
> Finally the news reached his father; and, hearing of Francis' reception at the hands of his fellow citizens, he hurried out to find him, not indeed to set him free, but to chastise him. Throwing moderation and discretion to the winds, he sprang on his son like a wolf on a lamb;

and, his face furious, his eyes glaring, he seized him with many blows and dragged him home. Francis was then shut up in a dark cellar, and for many days, his father used threats and blows to bend his son's will, to drag him back from the path of good he had chosen, and to force him to return to the vanities of the world.

All this strengthened Francis in alacrity to carry through his resolution, and he patiently endured the blows and hard words. When his father had to leave home on urgent business, his mother, who disapproved of her husband's action, reasoned gently with her son. But when she saw that nothing would move him from his good resolution, she was filled with tender pity, and, breaking his bonds, she set him free.

Giving thanks to almighty God, Francis went back to his former refuge; but he now enjoyed the greater liberty of one who had been tried and strengthened through having suffered trials and temptations.

Legend of the Three Companions, 18-19.

To see the Chiesa Nuova

After passing the first pillar on the left (A), you can see the "cell" where Francis was detained by his father. The wooden statue dates from the 17th century. Near the second left-hand pillar (B) there is a door marked Santuario; through this door

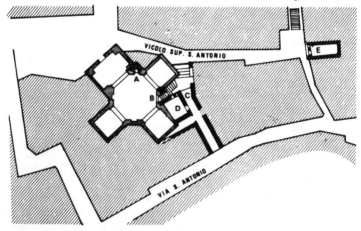

Chiesa Nuova and San Francesco Picolo. The oldest sections are in black.

you can visit the rest of St. Francis' house. There is the entrance to the house as well as what may be a "porta del morto". (See above, p. 14). There is also the ancient street (C) and the shop of Pietro di Bernardone (D).

At San Francesco Picolo (E)

You can see the remains of frescoes from the 13th to 15th centuries.

THE HOUSE of BERNARDO
DI QUINTAVALLE

It was two years since Francis had begun to lead a life of penance, and he was still alone. Bernardo di Quintavalle was the first to join him, and it was in this house that the first Franciscan vocation was decided.

> The truth of his teaching was brought home to people by the simplicity of his way of life, and two years after his own conversion, several men were drawn to follow his example of penitence, and they left everything in order to join him. The first of these was Brother Bernard of holy memory. He well knew how luxuriously Francis had lived in the world; therefore, when he saw how he labored to restore ruined churches and what a harsh life he led, Bernard too resolved to sell his possessions and give all to the poor. It seemed to him the will of God that he should follow Francis in clothing and his whole manner of life. With this in mind he went one day secretly to see God's servant and opened his heart to him, also inviting him to come that evening and lodge in his house.

> Francis joyfully gave thanks to God, because so far he had had no

companions and Master Bernard was a virtuous and godly man. Therefore, as arranged, he went to Bernard's house and remained there all night in great joy of heart. Bernard put a question to him: "If a man receives from God few or many possessions and, having enjoyed them for a number of years, now no longer wishes to retain them, what would be the best thing for him to do?" Blessed Francis answered that in that case it were better for the man to give back to God what he had received; to which Master Bernard rejoined; "Then, Brother, I will give all my worldly goods to the poor for love of God who gave them to me, according as you may think best". And Blessed Francis said to him: "Tomorrow early we will go to church; and as the Lord taught his disciples, we will learn from the book of the Gospel what to do".

Legend of the Three Companions, 27-28.

The house is located on **Via Bernardo di Quintavalle.** From the **Piazza del Comune** take **Via Portica** then turn left on **Via S. Gregorio.** Or, from **Piazza Vescovado**, go to the upper corner and take the left-hand street.

PORTA PERLICI

We now turn our attention to the ancient **Porta Perlici** which can be found at the end of **Via Porta Perlici.** An inscription indicates that it was built in 1199 to permit access to the Marches. Francis must have often passed through this gate, which was built in his youth. Especially noteworthy, however, is the fact that it was through this gate that he entered Assisi for the last time. It was then that the following episode took place:

> After his stay at Siena and at Le Celle di Cortona, blessed Francis returned to St. Mary of the Porziuncola and then went to stay at Bagnara, north of Nocera, where they had just built a house for the brothers; and he lived there for a certain time. But because his feet and legs had begun to swell due to his dropsy, his condition worsened. The people of Assisi were informed of this and immediately sent a few knights to this friary to bring him back to Assisi. They were in fact afraid to let him die there and in that case be forced to relinquish the possession of his holy body to others. The knights, therefore, brought the sick man back to Assisi.
>
> During the trip they stopped at a small market-town in the region of Assisi to eat. Blessed Francis stopped at the house of a man in that locality who received him with joy and charity. The knights went through the entire village to buy provisions: they found nothing. Returning to blessed Francis, they said to him, jokingly as it were: "Brother, you will have to give us some of your alms, for we found nothing to buy". Blessed Francis answered with great spiritual fervor: "If you found nothing it is because you placed your confidence in your flies, that is to say, in your pennies, and not in God. Go back to the houses you went to without shame; and instead of asking for merchandise to buy, ask alms for the love of God. The Holy Spirit will act in you, and you will find an abundance of everything".
>
> They went and asked for alms as the holy Father had recommended to them. Men and women gave them of what they had generously and joyfully. Overjoyed, they came back to find blessed Francis and told him what had happened. They considered the thing miraculous, for everything had transpired as he had predicted.

Legend of Perugia, 59.

Every year, on the Saturday before the first Sunday of September, a group of "knights" from Assisi goes to Satriano. Returning the following day in a make-believe cortege, the **Cavalcata**, they celebrate the "return of Francis".

THE PORZIUNCOLA

Once upon a time there were some woods, a footpath, and a little chapel, almost completely in ruins. The woods have been replaced by a city, the path by a road, and over the chapel there stands a magnificent basilica.

It is useless to regret these changes; in a way, they help to remind us that comtemporary spirituality does not permit us to return to the pristine days of Franciscan living. Our ascetism, however, can be to try to eliminate the "romantic" ideas from our consideration of this life, so that we can better grasp its essential elements.

A chapel in ruins

At San Damiano, Francis heard Christ's command: "Go and repair my house, which is in ruins". Interpreting these words materialistically, Francis successively repaired San Damiano and another chapel dedicated to St. Peter.

> Then he went to another place which is called the Portiuncola where there stood a church of the Blessed Virgin Mother of God that had been built in ancient times, but was now deserted and cared for by no one. When the holy man of God saw how it was thus in ruins, he was moved to pity, because he burned with devotion toward the mother of all good; and he began to live there in great zeal.

It was the third year of his conversion when he had finished repairing this church. At this time he wore a kind of hermit's dress, with a leather girdle about his waist; he carried a staff in his hands and wore shoes on his feet.

1 Celano, 21.

The Gospel "to the letter"

February 24, 1208. It was about three years since Francis had heard Christ's call; two years since he had renounced his possessions and left his family. He finished the work on the Porziuncola but, in reality, he didn't know exactly what he wanted – or rather, what God wanted!

But when on a certain day the Gospel was read in that church how the Lord sent his disciples out to preach, the holy man of God, assisting there, understood somewhat the words of the Gospel; after Mass he humbly asked the priest to explain the Gospel to him more fully. When he had set forth for him in order all these things, the holy Francis, hearing that the disciples of Christ should not possess gold or silver or money; nor carry along the way scrip, or wallet, or bread, or a staff; that they should not have shoes, or two tunics, but that they should preach the kingdom of God and penance, immediately cried out exultingly: "This is what I wish, this is what I seek, this is what I long to do with all my heart". Then the holy father, overflowing with joy, hastened to fulfill that salutary word he had heard, and he did not suffer any delay to intervene before beginning devoutly to perform what he had heard. He immediately put off his shoes from his feet, put aside the staff from his hands, was content with one tunic, and exchanged his leather girdle for a small cord. He designed for himself a tunic that bore a likeness to the cross, that by means of it he might beat off all temptations of the devil; he designed a very rough tunic so that by it he might crucify the flesh with all its vices and sins; he designed a very poor and mean tunic, one that would not excite the covetousness of the world. The other things that he had heard, however, he longed with the greatest diligence and the greatest reverence to perform. For he was not a deaf hearer of the Gospel, but committing all that he had heard to praiseworthy memory, he tried diligently to carry it out to the letter.

1 Celano, 22.

The Porziuncola, Mother and Head of the Order

Several years had passed. Bernard, Peter and Giles were soon followed by others who joined Francis. The first twelve friars went to Rome to ask the Lord Pope Innocent III to approve their way of life. New members began to come; the camping life-style of Rivotorto was no Longer possible. They had to begin to organize:

Seeing that God wanted to multiply the number of the brothers, one day blessed Francis said to them: "My dear brothers and sons, I see that the Lord wishes us to increase in number. In my opinion, it would be well and in conformity with religion to ask our bishop or the canons of St. Rufino, or the abbot of the monastery of St. Benedict for a small and poor church where the brothers may recite their Hours and, next to it, a small and poor house built of earth and wood where the brothers can sleep and go about their work. The place we are using is no longer suitable and the house too small, since it pleases the Lord to multiply us. Above all, we have no church where the brothers may recite their Hours; and were someone to die, it would not be fitting to bury him here nor in the church of the secular clerics". All the brothers agreed with him.

He then went and presented his request to the bishop. The latter answered, "Brother, I have no church to give you".

He then went to the canons of St. Rufino and made the same request to them; they answered as the bishop did.

Next, he went to the monatery of St. Benedict on Mount Subasio and made the same speech to the abbot as he did to the bishop and the canons, and told him the answer he had already received from the bishop and the canons. The abbot, moved with pity, took counsel with his brothers. God having so decided, they gave blessed Francis and his brothers the church of St. Mary of the Porziuncola, the poorest church they owned, for no poorer church could be found in the whole territory of the city of Assisi. This was what blessed Francis had long desired. The abbot said to blessed Francis: "Brother, we have granted your request. But it is our wish that, if the Lord multiplies your Order, this friary will be the head of all those you will found". These words were approved by blessed Francis and by all the brothers.

The saint was very happy that this place had been given to the brothers, because it was very poor, and also becáuse of its name of Porziuncola. The fact that it was called the church of the Porziuncola was indeed a presage that it would become the mother and head of the Order of the poor lesser brothers. The church had been given the name of Porziuncola because the aforesaid place where the church had been built had already been called Porziuncola for a very long time.

Blessed Francis said: "It was the Lord's will that no other church be given to the brothers nor did he allow the first brothers to build or possess another because this one was, as it were, a prophecy that is now fulfilled by the arrival of the lesser brothers". Although it was very poor and almost in ruins for a long time, the inhabitants of the afore-mentioned place and those of the city of Assisi always had a great devotion for this church, a devotion that has continued to grow even to this day.

As soon as the brothers arrived in this place to take up their residence, the Lord increased their number almost daily. The news of the brothers as well as their renown spread throughout all the valley of Spoleto.

Many years ago, before the people of the country had named St. Mary of the Porziuncola, this church had nevertheless been called St. Mary of the Angels; moreover, even after the brothers had begun to repair it, the men and women of that region still said: "Let us go to St. Mary of the Angels".

The abbot and his monks had given this church to blessed Francis and his brothers without any restriction: they had demanded no payment or yearly rent. Nevertheless, blessed Francis as a good and prudent master, wanted to build his house on solid rock and his Order on true poverty. And so, every year he sent a basket full of small fish, called loaches, to the monks. He did this as a sign of very great humility and poverty so that the brothers would not own any place as their own, or dwell in any place that was not the property of someone else, and so that they would not have the right either to sell or to alienate a property in any way whatsoever. And so each year the brothers brought their small fishes to the monks. Because of the humility of blessed Francis who did this because he wished them well, the monks in return offered him and his brothers the gift of a vessel full of oil.

Legend of Perugia, 8.

The Chapter of Mats

When he had obtained the church of St. Mary of the Angels from the abbot of Mt. Subasio, blessed Francis decided to hold two chapters a year there – at Pentecost and the feast of St. Michael (*Legend of the Three Companions*, 57). With the growth of the Order they had to change the Chapters, at first to one a year, then later to one every three years. But this event was still newsworthy enough to evoke some comment by Cardinal James of Vitry, who wrote in one of his letters:

> Once a year, in a place on which they agree, the men of this Order assemble to rejoice in the Lord and eat together; and they profit greatly from these gatherings. They seek the counsel of upright and virtuous men; they draw up and promulgate holy laws and submit them for approval to the Holy Father; then they disband again for a year and go about through Lombardy, Tuscany, Apulia, and Sicily.

The most famous chapter occurred in May of 1217 or 1219, and was attended by about 5,000 friars. These were housed in huts made of branches; hence the name, Chapter of Mats.

> Once the most faithful servant of Christ, St. Francis, held a General Chapter on the plain at St. Mary of the Angels, where more than five thousand friars gathered together. And St. Dominic, the head and founder of the Order of Friars Preacher, was also there with seven friars of his Order. He was at that time going from Bologna to Rome, and on hearing about the Chapter which St. Francis was holding on the plain at St. Mary of the Angels, he went to see it.
>
> There was also present at that Chapter the Lord Ugolino, Cardinal of Ostia, who was very devoted to St. Francis and his friars. St. Francis prophesied that he would be Pope, and so it happened: he was later the Pope called Gregory the Ninth. As the Court of the Lord Pope was then in Perugia, that Cardinal deliberately came to Assisi, and he used to come every day to see St. Francis and his friars, and sometimes he sang the Mass, and sometimes he gave a sermon to the friars at the Chapter.
>
> The Cardinal felt the greatest delight and inspiration when he came to visit that holy assembly and saw the friars sitting about on the plain around St. Mary's in groups of sixty or a hundred or two or three hundred, all occupied only in talking about God or in praying, weeping, or doing deeds of charity. And they were so quiet and meek that there was no sound or noise. And marveling at such a great crowd organized as an army camp, he would say with tears and great devotion: "Truly this is the camp and the army of the knights of God!".
>
> Indeed in all that throng no one was heard telling stories or jokes, but wherever a group of friars gathered, either they prayed or recited

the office, or they wept over their own sins or those of their benefactors, or they talked about the salvation of souls.

And in that camp each group had made tents covered on top and round about with rushes and mats; accordingly this Chapter was called the Chapter of Rushes or Mats. They slept on the bare ground or on some straw, and their pillows were stones or pieces of wood.

As a result, everyone who saw or heard them had such devotion for them, and the fame of their holiness was so great, that many people came to see them from the Pope's Court, which was then nearby at Perugia, and from other parts of the Valley of Spoleto. Many counts and barons and knights and other noblemen and many plain people, and cardinals and bishops and abbots with other members of the clergy, flocked to see this very holy and large and humble gathering of so many saintly men, such as the world has never seen. And they came especially to see the venerable leader and very saintly Father of all that company, who had stolen such beautiful prey from the world and had gathered such a fine and devout flock to follow in the footsteps of the true shepherd Jesus Christ.

When the entire General Chapter had assembled, St. Francis, the holy Father of all and Minister General, stood up and with fervor of spirit explained the word of God and of life to that holy flock, and – in a loud voice, as clear as a bugle, which divine unction gave him – preached to them whatever the Holy Spirit made him utter. And he took these words as the theme of his sermon: "My little sons, we have promised great things, but far greater things have been promised to us. Brief is the world's pleasure, but the punishment that follows it lasts forever. Small is the suffering of this life, but the glory of the next life is infinite". And preaching very devoutly on these words, he consoled and encouraged all the friars to reverence and obedience to Holy Mother Church and to sweet brotherly love, to pray for all the people of God, to have patience in the adversities of the world and temperance in prosperity, to maintain an angelic purity and chastity, to remain in peace and harmony with God and with all men and with their own conscience, to humility and meekness toward all; to the contempt of the world and a love and fervent practice of holy poverty, to care and attention in holy prayer and the praise of God, to place all their hope and anxiety for soul and body in the Good Shepherd who nourishes our bodies and souls: Our Blessed Lord Jesus Christ.

And then he said: "In order that you may better observe this, by merit of holy obedience I command all you friars who are gathered here that none of you is to have any care or anxiety concerning anything to eat or drink or the other things necessary for the body, but to concentrate only on praying and praising God. And leave all your worries about your body to Christ, because He takes special care of you".

And all of them received this order with joy in their hearts and on their faces. And when St. Francis ended his sermon, they all ran and gave themselves to prayer.

But St. Dominic, who was present, was greatly surprised at St. Francis' command and thought that he was proceeding in an imprudent way in ordering that not a single friar in such a large gathering should take any thought regarding things that are necesssary for the body, and he thought that such a great crowd would suffer as a result. But the Lord Jesus Christ wanted to show that He takes special care of His sheep and His poor, for by God's Providence it soon happened that He inspired the people of Perugia, Spoleto, Foligno, Spello, Assisi, and all the surrounding country to bring food and drink to that holy assembly. And all of a sudden men came from these places with many donkeys, mules, and wagons loaded with bread and wine, beans and cheese, and all other good things to eat which they thought these blessed poor men of Christ would need and could use. Moreover, they brought large and small pitchers and glasses and tablecloths and other things which such a crowd would need.

And whoever among them could bring the most supplies or serve most thoughtfully considered himself fortunate to provide for the needs of all in that holy gathering. And you could see the knights and noblemen who came to the meeting gladly and humbly and devoutly serving that assembly of saints. You could see members of the clergy faithfully and eagerly running everywhere like servants. You could see young men serving with so much reverence that it seemed as though they were serving, not the poor friars, but the Apostles of Our Lord Jesus Christ.

Therefore, when St. Dominic saw all this and realized that Divine Providence was acting through them, he humbly reproached himself for having misjudged St. Francis regarding the imprudent order, and he meekly knelt before him and accused himself of his fault, adding: "God is truly taking care of these holy little poor men, and I did not realize it. Therefore I promise henceforth to observe the holy poverty of the Gospel. And in the name of God I lay a curse upon all the friars of my Order who shall presume to have private property".

Thus St. Dominic was greatly edified by St. Francis' faith and the obedience and poverty of such a great and orderly assembly and by Divine Providence and the abundant supply of all good things. For as a truly saintly and wise man he acknowledged in all he said the perfectly faithful Lord who, just as He makes the lilies and plants of the fields grow and He nourishes the birds of the air, also furnishes everything that His devoted poor men need.

During that same Chapter St. Francis was told that many friars were wearing breastplates and iron rings on their flesh, and as a result some had become ill and some were dying, and others were hindered in praying. So St. Francis as a very wise Father commanded under holy obedience that whoever had a breastplate or an iron ring should take it off and deposit it before him. And they did so. And at least five hundred breastplates and many more iron rings worn on the arm or torso were found, and they formed a large pile. And St. Francis made the friars leave them there.

Later when the Chapter was over, St. Francis instructed and encouraged all of them to do good, and he taught them how to escape without sin from this evil world. And he sent them all back to their provinces comforted and filled with spiritual joy, with God's blessing and his own.

To the glory of our Lord Jesus Christ – may He be blessed! Amen.

Fioretti, 18.

The Porziuncola, model of the Order

Francis wanted the Porziuncola to serve as a model for the entire Order. The following story shows how much he wanted nothing to change that. It also shows how the behavior and feelings of the citizens of Assisi had changed since the time of his conversion.

What follows took place at the time of the chapter, for at that time it was held every year at St. Mary of the Porziuncola. By the grace of God, the brothers had multiplied and were multiplying every day. Now, all they had for the general gathering was a poor small hut covered with straw and a wall made of branches and mud, such as the brothers had built when they settled in that place. The inhabitants of Assisi noticed this and organized a group to come to their aid. In a few days and with much haste and fervor they built a large house made of stones cemented together, but without the consent of blessed Francis and in his absence.

When he returned for the chapter from the province where he was and saw the house they had built in that place, he was very astonished. Then he said to himself that this house would serve as an excuse for the brothers in the friaries where they lived or would live to erect or have erected large buildings. Since he desired that this friary should always be the model and the very pattern of all the fraternities, one day before the end of the chapter he got up, climbed on the roof of this house and ordered several brothers to climb up with him. With their help, he began to throw the tile with which the house was covered down to the ground, having decided to demolish it.

Some knights and other inhabitants of Assisi happened to be there. The commune had provided for a surveillance corps to protect the place against the lay people and outsiders who, having come from all over to see the chapter of the brothers, were massed near the friary. Seeing that blessed Francis and the other brothers wanted to destroy the house, they came closer and said to blessed Francis: "Brother, this house belongs to the commune of Assisi, and we are here to represent the commune; that is why we are telling you not to destroy this house". Blessed Francis answered them: "Well, if this house belongs to you, I do not want to touch it". He came down immediately, and so did the brothers who were with him.

That is why the people of Assisi for a long time decided that each year the podestà, whoever he was, would be obliged to see to it that the house had a roof and that the necessary repairs be made.

Legend of Perugia, 11.

(The foundations of this house can be seen beneath the main altar of the Basilica).

Brother Peter of Catanii

At the same time as Bernardo di Quintavalle, Peter Catanii joined Francis. Faithful companion of the first days, it was he whom Francis chose to replace him when, in 1218 (or 1220) he renounced the leadership of the Order.

Blessed Francis wanted to remain humble among his brothers. In order to preserve the greatest humility, he resigned his post as superior a few years after his conversion on the occasion of a chapter held at St. Mary of the Porziuncola. In the presence of all the brothers, he spoke as follows: "As of today and as far as you are concerned, I am dead. But here is Brother Peter Catanii whom all of us will obey". Then, all the brothers began to weep out loud and to shed abundant tears. Next, blessed Francis bowed before Brother Peter and promised to show him respect and obedience. From that time on, he was subject to him until his death, just as any one of the brothers.

Legend of Perugia, 105.

Brother Peter held that office for only a short time. He died on March 10, 1221, and was buried at the Porziuncola.

A New Testament

During the days that Peter Catanii led the Order, an insignificant event happened – but one that reveals the spirit of Francis as it was exeprienced at the Porziuncola.

> Another time when he was staying at St. Mary of the Porziuncola, a poor old woman whose two sons were in the Order came to the friary to ask blessed Francis for an alms; for that year she had nothing to live on. Blessed Francis said to Brother Peter Catanii who was at that time was Minister General: "Can we find something for our mother?" (For he said that the mother of a brother was his mother and the mother of all the brothers of the Order). Brother Peter answered: "We have nothing in the house we can give her especially in view of the fact that we would have to give her a rather sizeable alms to carry her through. However, there is a New Testament in the church from which we read the lessons at Matins". In those days, the brothers had no breviaries and only a few psalters. Blessed Francis answered: "Give our mother the New Testament; she will sell it to take care of her needs. I firmly believe that we will give greater pleasure to the Lord and to the Blessed Virgin his Mother by giving it to her than by reading it".
>
> And so they gave it to her.

Legend of Perugia, 56.

Sister Cricket

Francis loved all the animals, and, in almost all the places where he lived, there were some that he tamed. At the Porziuncola there was a cricket.

It was summer. Blessed Francis was then living at the friary of St. Mary of the Porziuncola in the last cell near the hedge of the garden behind the house where Brother Rayner the gardener lived after Francis' death. One day, as he was coming out of his cell, he saw a cricket within reach of his hand perched on the branch of a fig tree that was growing near the cell. He stretched out his hand and said: "Come, Sister Cricket". It immediately climbed his fingers. Meanwhile the saint caressed it with the other hand, saying to it: "Sing, Sister Cricket". It obeyed him at once and began to sing. This was a great consolation for the saint and he praised the Lord. He kept it in his hand that way for an hour. Then, he put it back on the branch from which he had taken it.

For eight days, each time the saint came out of his cell he found it in the same place, took it in his hands, and as soon as he told it to sing, it did. At the end of eight days, he said to his companions: "Let us now allow our sister cricket to go where she wants to. She has sufficiently delighted us and our flesh could find in her a reason for vainglory". Given permission to leave, the cricket then and there went away and was no longer seen. The companions admired her gentleness and obedience toward the saint. Blessed Francis found so much joy in creatures for love of the Creator that the Lord tamed the wild beasts to console the body and soul of his servant.

Legend of Perugia, 84.

The Porziuncola Indulgence

Francis especially loved the Porziuncola. It is said (*Legend of Perugia*, 9) that it was revealed to him in a dream that God had granted numerous prerogatives to this place. He wanted everyone to be able to participate in this and, for this reason he requested a special indulgence from the Holy See.

Francis got up early in the morning, called Brother Masseo and, with him, went and presented themselves to the Lord Pope. "Most Holy Father", he said, "I recently repaired a church in honor of the

Blessed Virgin, Mother of Christ. I ask your holiness to grant a special indulgence, without requiring any offering, in that church on the anniversary of its consecration".

The Pope replied: "I don't think that would be right, because the person requesting the indulgence should do something. But, tell me, how many years' indulgence would you like? One year? Do you want a three year indulgence?".

And St. Francis said, "But what's that?".

– "Well, what if I granted a six year indulgence?".

When he began talking about seven years, Francis was still not satisfied; "But, my Lord", he said, "what is that?".

– "What do you want me to do?".

– "Holy Father, please don't grant me years, but souls".

– "What do you mean by souls", asked the Pontiff.

– If it please Your Holiness, because of the favors God has granted this place, I ask that, whoever enters this place, having confessed their sins and, if necessary, being absolved by a priest, be freed from the guilt and punishment of all the sins that they have committed from the day of their baptism until the time they entered this church".

The Pope replied, "You are asking an awful lot; it is not the usual practice of the Holy See to grant such an indulgence".

– "My Lord", replied St. Francis, "it is not I who ask this but rather He who sent me, the Lord Jesus Christ".

And the Pope responded, "I will grant your request". And he repeated three times, "I grant your request; in the name of the Lord, let it be done".

When the cardinals who were there saw what had happened, they asked the Pope to revoke this privilege because it would harm the efforts in the Holy Land. But the Holy Father replied, "I cannot revoke this once I have granted it".

– "But, please consider it", the cardinals said, "such an indulgence will undermine the indulgences for the Crusades, it will depreciate the indulgences granted in honor of the Apostles Peter and Paul, which require more from the person seeking them".

– "We have already granted it", said the Pope, "we cannot, even if we wanted to, revoke what we have done".

– "At least reduce it in any way you can".

– "We could modify it somewhat", said the Pope, "by limiting it to one day".

He called Francis to him and said, "Behold, from this day forward, we grant that whoever comes to the above-mentioned church, confesses their sins and is truly contrite, will be delivered from all their guilt and punishment. However, it is our wish that this has effect for all time, but for one day a year, from first Vespers to Vespers of the following day, including the night".

Then, St. Francis, bowing his head, began to leave the palace. The Lord Pope, seeing him leaving, called after him and said, "Where are you going, my little man? What do you want as proof of this indulgence?"

And St. Francis replied, "Your word is enough for me. If this is God's will, He will make it known. I do not need any paper; the Virgin Mary is the parchment, Christ is my notary and the angels are my witnesses".

F. Bartholi, Tract. de Ind, Porz. ch. 6.

Brother Jacoba

There are only three women involved in the story of St. Francis: his mother, Clare, and Lady Jacoba dei Settesoli. The friendship of this woman with Francis and his Order never diminished.

Jacoba of Settesoli, equally renowned for her nobility and her sanctity in the city of Rome, had merited the privilege of a special love from St. Francis. It is not necesary for me to repeat unto her praise her illustrious origin, the dignity of her family, her great wealth, nor finally the wonderful perfection of her virtues, or her long continence as a widow. When therefore the saint lay in that illness that was to end all his suffering and bring to a most happy conclusion the happy course of his life, a few days before his death he wanted to send word to Rome for the Lady Jacoba, that if she wanted to see him whom she loved so ardently in this land of exile before he would go home to his fatherland, she should come with the greatest speed. A letter was written, a swift messenger was sought, and when one was found, he was gotten ready for the journey. Suddenly there was heard at the door the sound of horses, the noise of soldiers, and the crowd of a company of men. One of the companions, the one who had instructed the messenger, went to the door and found her there whom they had wanted to summon from afar. He was completely astonished, ran very quickly to the saint, and not being able to contain himself for joy, said: "I have something good to tell you, Father". And the saint immediately said in quick reply: "Blessed be God, who has guided the Lady Jacoba, our brother, to us. Open the door and bring her in, for our Brother Jacoba does not have to observe the decree against women".

There was a great rejoicing among the noble guests, and amid the rejoicing of spirit there was also a flowing of tears. And that nothing should be lacking to the miracle, the woman was found to have brought what the letter that had been previously written had contained about what should be brought for the father's burial. For God had seen to it that she brought the ashen-colored cloth with which to cover his dying body, also many candles, the cloth for his face, the little pillow for his head, a certain sweetmeat the saint had wanted to eat, and everything the spirit of this man had wanted. I want to tell the outcome of this true pilgrimage, lest I dismiss that noble pilgrim without consolation. A great multitude of nobles, especially the many devout people of the city, awaited the approaching birthday in death of the saint. But the saint was made stronger by the coming of these devout people from Rome, and it seemed for a little while that he would live a little longer. Wherefore that Lady ordered the rest of the company to leave, and only she herself with her children and a few attendants would remain. The saint said to her: "No, for I will depart on Saturday; on Sunday you may leave with all who have come with you".

3 Celano, 37-38

The death of Francis

Several steps away from the Porziuncola, but still inside the Basilica, is the chapel of the Transitus. This is where Francis died.

At last, when all God's mysteries had been accomplished in him, his holy soul was freed from his body and assumed into the abyss of God's glory, and Francis fell asleep in God. One of the friars, a disciple of his, saw his soul being borne on a white cloud over many waters to heaven, under the appearance of a radiant star. It shone with the brightness of sublime sanctity, full of the abundance of divine wisdom and grace which had earned for him the right to enter the home of light and peace, where he rests with Christ for ever.

The provincial minister of the friars in the Terra di Lavoro, Brother Augustine, a holy and upright man, was at death's door at that time. He had been unable to speak for some time, but now those who were with him suddenly heard him crying out, "Wait for me, father. Wait! I am coming with you". The friars were amazed and asked him to whom he was speaking. He replied, "Can't you see our father Francis. He is going to heaven". There and then his holy soul left his body and followed his father.

The bishop of Assisi was on a pilgrimage to the shrine of St.

Michael on Monte Gargano at that time, and St. Francis appeared to him on the night of his death, saying, "See, I am leaving the world and going to heaven". When he got up in the morning, the bishop told his companions the matter carefully and came to the conclusion that St. Francis left the world at the time he appeared to him in his vision.

At the time of St. Francis' death, when it was already dusk, a great flock of larks gathered over the building, although they normally prefer the light of day and avoid the shades of night. There they remained, flying about and singing with unusual joy, clearly testifying by the sweetness of their song to the glory of the saint who had so often called upon them to praise God.

St. Bonaventure, Legenda Major, XIV, 6.

To see Santa Maria degli Angeli

The construction of the Basilica was begun in 1569 to replace with one building the two that, until that time, had covered the Porziuncola and the place where Francis died. This basilica, impressive in its dimensions alone, fulfills the tasks given to its builders: protect the priceless Porziuncola and still contain the crowds that come for the great feasts. Without this basilica, the little chapel would probably not have lasted until today.

First we go to the **chapel of the Porziuncola** (A). The frescoes on the facade (Overbeck, 1829) merit only a glance. The interior, with its stones blackened by the smoke of votive lights, is touchingly simple. Behind the altar there is a large polyptych, the Annunciation and the History of the Porziuncola Indulgence, by Hilary of Viterbo (1393). The wooden door on the right dates from the 14th century. On the exterior, on the eastern wall is the memorial inscription to Peter Catanii (B) who died here in 1221. Beneath it, on the fragments of a 14th century fresco, the graffiti of 16th century pilgrims attests to the longevity of a terrible custom.

The cell where Francis died (C) is known as the little **chapel of the Transitus**. The fresco on the exterior wall (D. Bruschi, 1886) is of little interest. On the other hand, "The Companions of St. Francis" painted in the interior by Giovanni Spagna (1520) deserve our attention.

Passing through the door located on the left-hand side of the choir of the basilica (D), we can descend to the **crypt** of the sanctuary. Behind the altar is a beautiful tryptych by Della Robbia. At the end of the crypt, protected by a small cement wall, are the remains of the house (E) which the Assisi Co-mune built for the Chapter (see p. 39) and which Francis wanted to tear down.

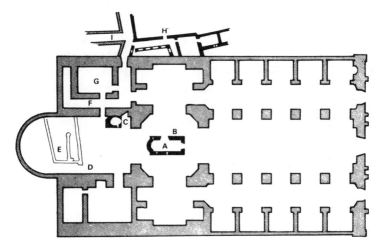

Basilica of Santa Maria degli Angeli. – (The oldest sections in black). – A: Chapel of the Porziuncola. – B: Memorial inscription of Peter Catanii. – C: Chapel of the Transitus. – D: Entrance to the crypt. – E: (in the crypt) the foundations of the Chapter House. – F: corridor. – G: Sacristy. – H: Mu-seum and convent of San Bernardino. – I: Passage toward the *Roseto*.

Leaving the crypt by the corridor (F) go to the **sacristy** (G) to see the wooden furniture carved by Brother James of Borgo San Sepolcro (1671).

Leaving the basilica by way of the corridor near the sacristy, notice, on the right, the remains of the **primitive convent** built in the 13th-15th century.

Enter the **museum** (H) which contains several interesting things, including a crucifix by Giunta Pisano (ca. 1236). A flight of stairs leads to a level where you can see some of the cells of the primitive convent.

Follow the signs to the **Roseto**: Francesco Bartholi (*Tractatus del Indulgenzia de la Porziuncola*, chapter 8) tells the story how, when Francis was spending the night here in prayr, he was tormented by demons. Francis rolled in the brambles here in the woods near the Porziuncola. Immediately the brambles were turned into thornless rose bushes. The roses of the Roseto, still thornless, have tinges of red, like drops of blood, on their leaves. They say that these are the descendants of the brambles that grew there in Francis' day.

On the side, a statue commemorates the niche of "Sister Cricket" (see p. 41). Further down the corridor there is the **Chapel of the Roses**, erected by St. Bonaventure to mark the site of a hut frequented by St. Francis. This chapel is decorated with a cycle of frescoes attributed to Tiberias of Assisi (1506-1516); the picture depicting Francis announcing the Porziuncola Indulgence is interesting because it shows the buildings which were on this site in the 16th century.

RIVO TORTO

Where exactly was Rivo Torto, this place that is filled with moving memories of the beginnings of the Franciscan Order? We will probably never know for certain. The sanctuary which bears this name today dates back to the 19th century. The stone huts there today are only pious, although imaginative reconstructions. The country side has changed; the forest has disappeared. The only authentic thing remaining is the serpentine brook (rivo torto) crossing the plain; in its waters the first friars washed their feet. That should suffice to help us think about the little fraternity which formed here around Francis.

A narrow hut

The first twelve Franciscans went to Rome and received the Pope's confirmation of their way of life (1209). On their return they settled at Rivo Torto where, apparently, Francis had already spent some time.

> The blessed father was then living with his sons in an abandoned and derelict hut at Rivo Torto, near Assisi. The place was so cramped that they could hardly sit or lie down to sleep; and very often for lack of bread their only food was turnips, for which, in their poverty, they begged here and there.
>
> Blessed Francis wrote the brothers' names on the beams of the hut so that each one, when he wished to sit or pray, should know his own place, and that no unnecessary noise due to the close quarters should disturb the brothers' quiet of mind.
>
> *Legend of the Three Companions, 55.*

Penance and discretion

An episode in the life of the little Franciscan fraternity at Rivo Torto makes us aware of Francis' remarkable discretion and courtesy.

> In the early days of the Order, that is to say, at the time when

Francis began to group a few brothers around him, he lived with them at Rivo Torto. One night around midnight, when all were sleeping on their poor straw matresses, one of the brothers began to cry out: "I am dying! I am dying!" Blessed Francis got up and said: "Get up, Brothers; bring a light!" A torch was lit and blessed Francis asked: "Who cried out: I am dying?"

One brother said, "I did".

And blessed Francis said to him: "What ails you, Brother? What are you dying from?".

"I am dying of hunger", he answered.

Blessed Francis, a man full of charity and discretion, did not want the brother to blush from eating alone. He had a meal prepared then and there and everyone partook of it. It must be said that this brother and the others with him were recently converted and inflicted excessive penances on their bodies.

After the meal, blessed Francis said to the other brothers: "My brothers, I say to you, let everyone of you take his constitution into consideration. If one of you can do with less food than another, it is not my wish that he who needs to eat more should try to imitate the first. Let each one take his own constitution into account and give his body what it needs. If, in the matter of eating and drinking we are obliged to deny ourselves those superfluous things which are harmful to the body and the soul, we must forego even more so excessive mortification, for God desires loving kindness and not sacrifice". He added: "My dear brothers, it was my wish that out of love for my brother all of us should partake of his meal so that he would not blush: we did so out of love and because he greatly needed it. I warn you, I will not do this again, for it would be neither religious nor upright. Rather it is my desire and command that each and everyone, while respecting our poverty, give his body what it needs".

Legend of Perugia, 1.

Brother Giles

It was at Rivo Torto that Giles, the third follower of Francis, joined the Order.

At the beginning of the Order, when he was living at Rivo Torto with only two friars, a man named Giles, who became the third friar, came to him from the world in order to share his way of life. And when he had remained there for some days, still wearing his secular clothes, a poor man came to the place asking alms of blessed Francis.

Turning to Giles, blessed Francis said to him, "Give this poor brother your cloak". At once Giles gladly removed it from his back and gave it to the poor man. Then it became clear to him that God had imparted a new grace to his heart, since he had given his cloak to the poor man with great cheerfulness. So he was received into the Order by blessed Francis, and constantly advanced in virtue to the greatest perfection.

Mirror of Perfection, 36.

Brother Fly

Not all of those coming to the new-born fraternity were motivated by the desire for true conversion. The *Legend of Perugia* has kept alive the memory of one lazy friar whom Francis had to dismiss.

> Blessed Francis often said that no brother should spend a long time without going out to beg. The more noble and great a brother was in the world the more the holy father was delighted and edified to see him go on the quest and perform servile work to give good example.
>
> That is what was done formerly. In the early days of the Order, when the brothers lived at Rivo Torto, there was a brother who prayed little and did no work, who never went begging, for he was ashamed, but he ate well. Considering his behavior, blessed Francis was warned by the Holy Spirit that this brother was a sensual man. One day he said to him: "Go your way, Brother Fly, for you wish to eat the fruit of the labor of your brothers, while you remain idle in the vineyard of God. You resemble Brother Drone who gathers nothing, does no work, but eats the fruit of the activity of the working bees". He left without even asking forgiveness, for he was a sensual man.

Legend of Perugia, 62.

Emperor Otto

Crossing the duchy of Spoleto, Otto IV passed by Assisi. He was probably travelling along the **Via Antica**, which passed within a half kilometer of Rivo Torto.

Traces of the road can be seen among the paths that cut across the fields. It was a great temptation to go and enjoy the spectacle.

He taught them not only to mortify vices and repress carnal movements, but also to restrain the exterior senses themselves, for through them death enters the soul. When at that time the Emperor Otto was passing through the place with much clamor and pomp to receive the crown of his earthly empire, the most holy father, who was living with his brothers in that hovel close to the road on which the emperor would pass, did not even go out to watch; and he did not let anyone else do so except one who continuously called out to the emperor that his glory would last but a short time, for the glorious saint, withdrawn within himself and walking in the broadness of his heart, had prepared within himself a dwelling fit for God, and therefore the outward clamor did not catch his ears, nor could any sound drive out or interrupt the great business he had at hand. The apostolic authority was strong in him, and he therefore refused entirely to offer flattery to kings and princes.

1 Celano, 43.

Evicted by a donkey

Things had gone well at Rivo Torto and the little fraternity would have gladly stayed there.

However, it wasn't to be in this place that the Order would take roots; and it was a donkey that taught the brothers this.

One day while they were still living in this place, a peasant came along driving his donkey with the intention of taking possession of the hut. Fearing that the brothers might protest, he drove the donkey straight in, saying: "In with you, in with you; this place will just do for us". When the blessed Father heard the words and realized the peasant's intention, he was considerably annoyed, especially because the commotion caused by the man and his donkey had disturbed the brothers intent upon silent prayer. So he turned to them: "Dear Brothers, I know that God has not called me to entertain a donkey and live in the company of men, but to show men the way of salvation by preaching and wise counsel. We must, therefore, above all, make sure of being able to pray and give thanks for the graces we receive".

So they left the hut which later was used by poor lepers, and they moved to Saint Mary of the Angels, the Porziuncola; nearby was a little dwelling in which they lived before they received the church itself.

Legend of the Three Companions, 55.

LA ROCCA

The fortress we see today was reconstructed in the 14th century on the foundations of the one dismantled by the Assisians in 1198. Francis, then a young man of 18, was probably among them. The ruins are a fine specimen of military architecture and can evoke for us the rivalries between the Pope and the Emperor, between Assisi and Perugia, or between the **maggiori** and **minori**.

This site, however, also serves as a fantastic observation point from which we can see numerous places whose names recur in the biographies of St. Francis.

Running from east to west there **is Mount Subasio**; on its flank is the road to the **Carceri**. Higher and to the right are the ruins of the abbey of **Saint Benedict**. It was here that the abbot granted Francis the use of the Porziuncola in exchange for a basket of fish (see p. 31).

In the distance (east) are **Spello** and **Foligno**, where Francis went to sell the cloth to obtain money for the repair of **San Damiano**. San Damiano can easily be recognized because of the distinctive cypresses which surround it.

On the plain below is the sanctuary of **Rivo Torto**; beyond it, at the foot of the distant hills, between **Bevagna** and **Cannara**, we have the site where Francis preached to the birds (*Fioretti*, 16).

On the plain below is the Basilica of **Santa Maria degli Angeli**, which houses the Porziuncola; on the other side of the valley is **Bettona** where the inhabitants, along with those of Assisi, thought that the woods of the **Porziuncola** were on fire. Closer

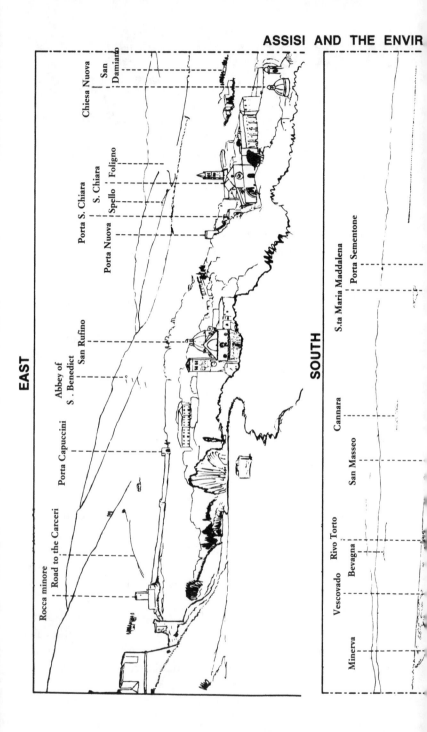

EAST

Rocca minore
Road to the Carceri
Porta Capuccini
Abbey of
S . Benedict
San Rufino
Porta Nuova
Porta S. Chiara
Spello
S. Chiara
Foligno
Chiesa Nuova
San Damiano

SOUTH

Minerva
Bevagna
Vescovado
Rivo Torto
San Masseo
Cannara
S.ta Maria Maddalena
Porta Sementone

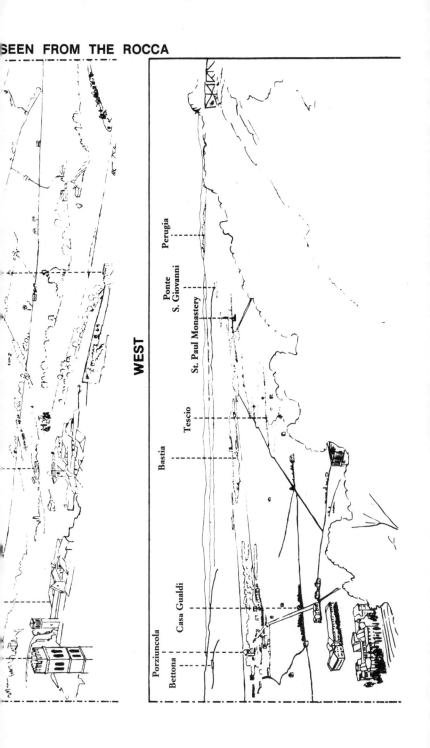

WEST

Perugia

Ponte
S. Giovanni

St. Paul Monastery

Tescio

Bastia

Porziuncola

Bettona

Casa Gualdi

investigation, however, revealed that it was the great light that surrounded Francis and Clare who were sharing a meal together (*Fioretti*, 15).

Farther in the same direction, but closer to Assisi at the crossroads is the **Casa Gualdi** where the leprosarium once stood; it was from here that Francis blessed the city for the last time.

On the heights of **Bastia**, near the confluence of the Tescia and the Chiascio Rivers was the **Monastery of St. Paul**, where Francis took Clare after she received the habit. The church is now part of a cemetery.

Farther to the west lies **Ponte San Giovanni** where Francis was taken prisoner in 1202 during the war between Assisi and Perugia.

Finally, in the distance, is **Perugia**, where Francis was held captive for a year (*Legend of the Three Companions*, 4).

At the foot of **La Rocca** there lies the whole of **Assisi** from **San Rufino** where Francis was baptized to San Francesco where he is immortalized.

The herald of the great king

From the other side of the large wall that runs the length of the Rocca, there is a fantastic view of the **Tescio** Valley. A small road descends to the left of the cemetery and crosses the Tescio on an old bridge, **Ponte Santa Croce**, formerly known as **Ponte dei Galli**, the Bridge of the Frenchmen. On the other side of the river the road climbs again; at the point where it makes a sharp turn, the following episode took place as Francis was leaving Assisi after his renunciation at the Bishop's Palace.

> Now that he was free from the bonds of all earthly desires in his disregard for the world, Francis left the town and sought out a place where he could be alone, without a care in the world. There in solitude and silence he would be able to hear God's secret revelations.
>
> Then as he was walking through the forest joyfully singing in French and praising God, he was suddenly set upon by robbers. They threatened him and asked him who he was but he replied intrepidly

with the prophetic words, "I am the herald of the great King". Then they beat him and threw him into a ditch full of snow, telling him, "Lie there, rustic herald of God". With that they made off and Francis jumped from the ditch, full of joy, and made the woods re-echo with his praise to the Creator of all.

Legenda Major, II, 5.

On the preceding pages there are sketches of the view from the Rocca.

SAN DAMIANO

In spite of the inevitable repairs and improvements over the centuries, San Damiano remains essentially as it was in the time of St. Francis. For this reason it is important to spend some time here.

The voice of the crucifix

It is autumn of 1205 and Francis, in whose soul grace has begun to work, for the first time enters the little church of San Damiano. During his prayer, he seems to hear the large Byzantine crucifix speak to him (The original crucifix is now in the Basilica of Santa Chiara).

> While he was walking near the church of San Damiano, an inner voice bade him go in and pray. He obeyed, and kneeling before an image of the crucified Savior, he began to pray most devoutly. A tender, compassionate voice then spoke to him: "Francis do you not see that my house is falling into ruin? Go, and repair it for me". Trembling and amazed Francis replied: "Gladly I will do so, O Lord". He had understood that the Lord was speaking of that very church which, on account of its age, was indeed falling into ruin.
>
> These words filled him with the greatest joy and inner light because in spirit he knew that it was indeed Jesus Christ who had spoken to him.
>
> *Legend of the Three Companions, 13.*

A difficult lesson

When Francis heard the crucifix, there were only the church, a few small buildings and the wing where the refectory now stands. The church was run-down and the poor priest who served this country church hardly had the means to manage its necessary upkeep. To Francis, the message was clear; he had to repair that church. (However, the message didn't really refer to that little church, but to the entire Church). Nevertheless, repairing a church takes money and, when you are the son of Pietro di Bernardone, you know how to get it.

> Filled with joy at the vision and words of Christ Crucified, Francis took various pieces of cloth of different colors for sale in the city of Foligno, and he sold not only the wares, but also the horse he was riding. He then returned to the church of Saint Damian, found the poor priest, and humbly kissing his hands, told him of what he proposed to do.
>
> The priest was astounded at Francis' sudden conversion and at first he did not believe in it. Thinking Francis to be joking, he refused the proffered money, and this was due to the fact that not long before he had seen Francis having a good time with his relatives and friends.
>
> Francis insisted more urgently and begged the priest to receive him as a guest for love of God. Finally the priest consented to his staying on, but, for fear of Francis' relatives, he would on no account accept the money; whereupon Francis threw the coins in through the window, so truly had he come to despise all gain.
>
> While Francis was staying in the priest's house, his father went round inquiring for news of his son. When he heard what had happened and where Francis was, calling together his friends and neighbors, he hurried off to find him.
>
> *Legend of the Three Companions, 16.*

Working for God

Obviously, God isn't satisfied when a person thinks he can take care of everything with money, especially when that money isn't come by honestly. He wanted Francis to give of himself. And so, Francis goes through the streets of Assisi, begging for stones and oil (see p. 105); we see him also on the scaffolds, working with the masons.

While working there with other men, he called out loudly and joy-fully in French to the passers-by: "Come and help us do this work for the church of Saint Damian which will become a monastery of women whose life and fame will cause our heavenly Father to be universally glorified".

In these words filled with the spirit of prophecy, he foretold the future, for this is the holy place in which the excellent order of the Poor Ladies and holy virgins was to flourish. This came about some six years after the conversion of blessed Francis, and their excellent manner of life and glorious institution was duly approved by the Lord Pope Gregory IX of blessed memory, at that time Bishop of Ostia; and his decision was confirmed by the authority of the Apostolic See.

Legend of the Three Companions, 24.

Clare at San Damiano

It was six years later, in 1212, that Francis' prophecy was fulfilled. Clare, following Francis' example, decided to follow Christ and, on Palm Sunday Francis received her into the Order at the Porziuncola; from there he took her to the abbey of San Paolo near Bastia.

Several days later she left for Sant'Angelo de Panzo; but as it was impossible to find peace of soul there, with the advice of St. Francis she returned to San Damiano. It was there that she cast anchor, and she never gave another thought to changing her residence. She had no more fear of solitude or of confinement in that place. This was the church which Francis had cared so much about and had given the priest the money to restore it. It was in this church, while praying, that Francis heard the voice from the crucifix calling to him, "Francis, go repair my house which, as you see, is falling in ruins". In the confines of this cloister the Virgin Clare enclosed herself for love of the heavenly Bridegroom. Here she took shelter against the storms of the world and spent her whole life as a prisoner. In this cave of mortification the silver dove chose to build her nest; it was here that the community of virgins was born; it was here that the Order of Poor Ladies began.

Celano, Vita S. Chiara, Ch. 5.

The Canticle of Creatures

Clare and Agnes, soon joined by others, formed the first community of Poor Ladies. In the beginning of 1225, Francis, suffering from various illnesses as well as from the painful stigmata, came to spend some time at San Damiano; here he wrote the **Canticle of the Creatures**.

Two years before his death, already very sick and suffering especially from his eyes, he was living in a cell made of mats at San Damiano. The minister general, seeing that his case was serious, ordered him to accept help and care. Moreover, he told him that he wanted to be present when the doctor began the treatment in order to see to it that he received the proper care and to comfort him, for he was suffering greatly. But at that time it was very cold and the weather was not propitious to begin the treatment.

During his stay here for fifty days and more, blessed Francis could not bear the light of the sun during the day or the light of the fire at night. He constantly remained in darkness inside the house in his cell. His eyes caused him so much pain that he could neither lie down nor sleep, so to speak, which was very bad for his eyes and for his health. A few times he was on the point of resting and sleeping, but in the house and in the cell made of mats, that had been made ready for him, there were so many mice running around here and there, around him and even on him, that they prevented him from taking a rest; they even hindered him greatly in his prayer. They annoyed him not only at night but also during the day. When he ate, they climbed up on the table, so much so that he and his companions were of the opinion that is was a diabolical intervention, which it was.

One night, as he was thinking of all the tribulations he was enduring, he felt sorry for himself and said interiorly: "Lord, help me in my infirmities so that I may have the strengh to bear them patiently!" And suddenly he heard a voice in spirit: "Tell me, Brother: if, in compensation for your sufferings and tribulations you were given an immense and precious treasure: the whole mass of the earth changed into pure gold, pebbles into precious stones, and the water of the rivers into perfume, would you not regard the pebbles and the waters as nothing compared to such a treasure? Would you not rejoice?". Blessed Francis answered: "Lord, it would be a very great, very precious, and in estimable treasure beyond all that one can love and desire!". "Well, Brother", the voice said, "be glad and joyful in the midst of your infirmities and tribulations: as of now, live in peace as if you were already sharing my kingdom".

The next morning on rising, he said to his companions: If the emperor gave a kingdom to one of his servants, how joyful the servant would be! But if he gave him the whole empire, would he not rejoice all the more? I should, therefore, be full of joy in my infirmities and tribulations, seek my consolation in the Lord, and give thanks to God the Father, to his only Son our Lord Jesus Christ, and to the Holy Spirit. In fact, God has given me such a grace and blessing that he has condescended in his mercy to assure me, his poor and unworthy servant, still living on this earth that I would share his Kingdom. Therefore, for his glory, for my consolation, and the edification of my neighbor, I wish to compose a new 'Praises of the Lord', for his creatures. These creatures minister to our needs every day; without them we could not live; and through them the human race greatly offends the Creator. Every day we fail to appreciate so great a blessing by not praising as we should the Creator and dispenser of all these gifts". He sat down, concentrated a minute, then cried out: "Most high, all-powerful, and good Lord ...". And he composed a melody to these words which he taught his companions.

His heart was then full of so much sweetness and consolation that he wanted Brother Pacificus, who in the world had been the king of poets and the most courtly master of song, to go through the world with a few pious and spiritual friars to preach and sing the praises of God. The best preacher would first deliver the sermon; then all would sing the "Praises of the Lord", as true jongleurs of God. At the end of the song, the preacher would say to the people: "We are the jongleurs of God, and the only reward we want is to see you lead a truly penitent life". Then he added: "Who are, indeed, God's servants if not jongleurs who strive to move men's hearts in order to lead them to the joys of the spirit?". When he spoke in this way of the servants of God, he especially had in mind the Friars Minor who had been given to the world to save it.

He called these "Praises of the Lord", which opened with the words: "Most high, all-powerful, and good Lord", the "Canticle of the Sun". The sun was the most beautiful of all the creatures, the one which, better than all the others, could be compared to God. He said: "At sunrise, every man ought to praise God for having created this heavenly body which gives light to our eyes during the day; at evening, when night falls, every man ought to praise God for that other creature, our brother fire, which enables our eyes to see clearly in the darkness. We are all like blind people, and it is through these two creatures that God gives us light. Therefore, for these two creatures and for the others that serve us each day, we ought to praise their glorious Creator in a very special way". He himself did so with all his heart, whether sick or well, and he gladly invited the others to sing the glory of the Lord. When he was laid low by sickness, he often intoned this canticle and had his companions take it up; in that way he forgot the intensity of his sufferings and pains by considering the glory of the Lord. He did this until the day of his death.

At the time when he was very sick – the "Praises of the Lord", had already been composed – the bishop of Assisi excommunicated the podestà. In return, the podestà had it announced to the sound of the trumpet in the streets of the city that every citizen was forbidden to buy from or sell anything whatsoever to the bishop or to transact any business with him. There was a savage hatred between them. Blessed Francis, who was very sick at that time, pitied them. It pained him to see that no one, religious or lay, intervened to reestablish peace and concord between them. So he said to his companions: "It is a great shame for us, the servants of God", that at a time when the podestà and the bishop so hate each other no one can be found to reestablish peace and concord between them! On this occasion he added the following strophe to his canticle:

All praise be yours, my Lord,
Through those who grant pardon for love of you;
Through those who endure sickness and trial.
Happy those who endure in peace;
By you, Most High, they will be crowned.

He then called one of his companions and said to him: "Go and find the podestà and tell him for me that he should go to the bishop's palace with the notables of the commune and with all those he can assemble". When the brother had left, he said to the others: "Go, and in the presence of the bishop, of the podestà, and of the entire gathering, sing the Canticle of Brother Sun. I have confidence that the Lord will put humility and peace in their hearts and that they will return to their former friendship and affection".

When everyone had gathered at the place of the cloister of the bishop's palace, the two brothers stood up, and one of them was the spokesman: "Despite his sufferings, blessed Francis", he said, "has composed the 'Praises of the Lord' for all his creatures, to the praise of God and for the edification of his neighbor; he asks you to listen with great devotion".

With that, they began to sing. The podestà stood up and joined his hands as for the Gospel of the Lord, and he listened with great recollection and attention; soon tears flowed from his eyes, for he had a great deal of confidence in blessed Francis and devotion for him. At the end of the canticle, the podestà cried out before the entire gathering: "In truth I say to you, not only do I forgive the lord bishop whom

I ought to recognize as my master, but I would even pardon my brother's and my own son's murderer!" He then threw himself at the feet of the lord bishop and said to him: "For the love of our Lord Jesus Christ and of blessed Francis, his servant, I am ready to make any atonement you wish". The bishop stood up and said to him: "My office demands humility of me, but by nature I am quick to anger; you must forgive me!" With much tenderness and affection, both locked arms and embraced each other.

Legend of Perugia, 42-44.

Clare's farewell to Francis.

In the mid-summer of 1225, Francis left San Damiano for Rieti to have his eyes treated. Clare and her sisters would never see him alive again.

During the week in which blessed Francis died, Lady Clare, the first little plant of the Order of Sisters, abbess of the Poor Ladies of San Damiano of Assisi, emulator of St. Francis in the continual observance of the poverty of the Son of God, was also very sick and was fearful of dying before blessed Francis. She wept bitterly and could not console herself at the thought of not seeing him again before his death, her only father next to God, her interior and external comfort, he who was the first one to establish her solidly in the grace of the Lord. She made this known to the saint through the intermediary of a brother.

On hearing this, Francis was moved with compassion; for he loved Clare and her sisters with a paternal affection for the saintly life they were leading and because it was he who with the grace of God had converted her by his advice, shortly after the arrival of the first brothers. Her conversion greatly edified not only the Order of the brothers but the whole Church. Since Francis could not grant her desire to see him again, because both of them were sick, he sent her in writing, for her consolation, his blessings and absolution from all the infractions of his orders and desires, and of the orders and desires of the Son of God. Furthermore, to rid her of all sadness and console her in the Lord, he said to the brother she had sent, or rather the Holy Spirit said it through his mouth: "Go and bring this letter to Lady Clare. You will tell her to banish the sorrow and sadness she experiences at the thought of never seeing me again. Let her know, in truth, that before she dies she and all her sisters will see me again and will receive great consolation from me".

A short while later, blessed Francis died during the night. In the morning, the people of Assisi, men and women and all the clergy, came in search of his body in the friary. To the chant of hymns and canticles, holding green palms in their hands, they bore him by the will of God to San Damiano, so that the word the Lord had spoken by the mouth of his saint might be fulfilled and that his daughters and servants might be consoled. The iron grill of the window through which the sisters received Holy Communion and heard the word of God was pulled back; the brothers lifted up the body of blessed Francis from the stretcher and held it in their arms before the opening for at least a minute. Lady Clare and her sisters experienced a very great consolation from this. Nevertheless they wept bitterly and felt great pain; for, next to God, the holy Father was their one and only consolation in this world.

Legend of Perugia, 109.

The Saracens are routed

Clare lived 27 years after Francis' death. Her community flourished; other convents had been founded. But at San Damiano, life outside the city walls was very dangerous. That was proven in September of 1240:

During those troubled times which afflicted the Church during the reign of the Emperor Frederick, the Spoleto valley frequently had to accept the chalice of divine wrath. Bands of mercenaries paid by the Emperor as well as bands of Saracen archers swarmed like bees into the region. They destroyed castles and looted the cities.

One day they came against Assisi, the city which the Lord especially loved; the army was already against the gates. The infamous tribe of Saracens, thirsting for Christian blood, was ready to commit any crime or act of audacity and had already penetrated the outer wall of San Damiano and had entered the cloister. The poor ladies were overcome with anguish and, their voices trembling with fright, they ran to take refuge around their mother. Clare, however, was not afraid; although ill herself, she asked to be taken to the cloister door and to have placed there as her only protection against the Saracens the ivory-covered silver pyx wherein was kept the Body of Christ.

She knelt in prayer before the Lord and with many tears prayed to Him, "Could it be your will, oh Lord, to deliver your servants whom you have nourished in your love into the hands of pagans? Guard them, oh Lord, for in his hour I am unable to take care of them".

From the ciborium, defender of the new covenant, the voice of a child was heard, "I will care for you always". Clare continued, "Lord, if it is your will, please protect this city, which continues to live in your love". And Christ replied, "It will suffer much, but I will come to its aid and protection".

Then the holy abbess, raising her tear-filled face, comforted her sisters, saying, "Indeed, my daughters, I assure you we will not be harmed. Simply have confidence in Christ". At that very moment the frenzy of those dogs was changed into fear and they climbed down the walls faster than they had scaled them; the power of that prayer had cast fear into their ranks. Bur Clare firmly enjoined the Sisters who had heard the voice, "My dearest daughters, as long as I am alive, make certain that you tell no one of this voice".

Celano, Vita S. Chiara, Ch. 21-22.

The city officials commemorate this **event annually** on June 22 with a procession to San Damiano; there they offer candles in memory of the city's deliverance from the Saracens.

The corporals embroidered by St. Clare

Francis, who had a special reverence for the Body of Christ, in several letters expressed his concern for the condition of sacred objects. Clare shared this concern and she embroidered many corporals. All of the testimony taken during her Process of Canonization recounts that fact, and they give us a vivid portrait of Clare:

She also told that once when Saint Clare was ill and could not rise from her bed, she asked for a certain cloth, and there being no one at that moment to bring it, a little cat of the monastery started to drag the cloth along the floor as best she could to bring it to Saint Clare, who seeing this said to the little cat: "O you bad one, you don't know to carry it; why do you drag it along the ground in that way?" Then the little cat, seeming to have understood those words, began to roll up the cloth so that it no longer touched the floor. Asked how she knew this, she said that Saint Clare herself had told her of it.

Sister Francesca said that she had herself counted fifty pairs of corporals made from the thread spun by Saint Clare; and these were distributed to churches as the other aforesaid sisters had described.

Process of Canonization, Witness 9.

Saint Clare, patroness of television

St. Clare was named patroness of television. In his life of St. Clare, Thomas of Celano shows us the reason for this choice:

> On Christmas Day, at the very hour when the Divine Child was born, when the world shares in the joy of the angels, all of the sisters had gone to the choir to pray Matins, abandoning their mother who was disabled by illness. She, however, began to think of the Infant Jesus, and was extremely afflicted because she was not able to join in his praises. She sighed, "My Lord God, behold I am left here alone". Suddenly the melodious concert with which the church of San Francesco was resounding came to her ears. She heard the joyous psalmody of the friars, the harmony of the chants; she even heard the sound of the organ. The church was not close enough for her to hear that singing; God himself must have either miraculously amplified the sounds of that ceremony or strengthened the hearing of the saint. But, an even greater miracle occurred, for she merited to see the Lord's manger. The following morning her daughters came to see her and St. Clare said, "Blessed be my Lord Jesus Christ who did not abandon me even when you were all gone. By his grace I was allowed to participate in the entire service at the Church of San Francesco".

Celano, Vita S. Chiara, Ch. 18.

The Franciscans at San Damiano

A community of women could not live in security so far outside the city walls; the episode with the Saracens, among others, proved that. For that reason the Clares were persuaded to leave San Damiano and move into the city. When Clare died in 1253 they buried her in San Giorgio, where Francis had been buried from 1226 to 1230. They began to build a Basilica in honor of Saint Clare and a monastery for the Poor Ladies. There were some obstacles to overcome and it was in 1257 that the sisters left San Damiano and moved to the new monastery.

San Damiano was not left empty; the Friars Minor soon moved in and remain there to this day.

To see San Damiano

A visit to San Damiano does not require a lot of commentary. Even its simplicity is inspiring.

1. Facade

The portico in front of the church and the buildings to the front, left and right, date to the 16th Century.

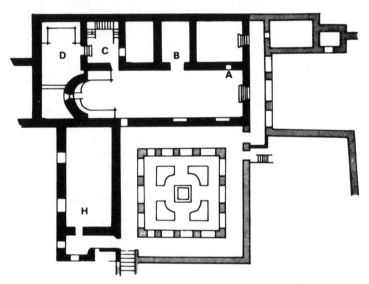

San Damiano (Ground floor). – The original buildings are in black. – A: "Finestra del denaro"; B: Chapel with the Crucifix of Innocent of Palermo; C: Cemetery chapel; D: Sister's Choir; H: Refectory.

To the left of the rose window and a little below it there is a door which leads to the sisters' dormitory. This door is really the old entrance to the monastery, situated above ground for the reasons given in the section on the doors of the dead (see p. 13). One entered by a wooden stairway suspended on chains. In 1253, upon the death of Clare's sister Agnes, so many people were standing on the stairway waiting to view the body that the chains broke and the stairs fell; fortunately, there were no serious injuries. (Chronicle of the 24 Generals, p. 178). A romantic (but false) tradition says that it was from this door that

Clare, holding the Blessed Sacrament, routed the Saracens. The truth is that Clare knelt in front of the Blessed Sacrament, which had been placed in front of the closed door. The testimony of Sister Francesa during the Process of Canonization tells us that it was the refectory door.

2. Church

On the right of the entrance (A) is a recess known as the "finestra del denaro"; here Francis left the purse of money which, the priest of San Damiano did not want to accept (see p. 58). The 14th century fresco which surrounds it shows (left) Francis in prayer before the Crucifix; (right) Francis is dragged away by his father in front of the terror-stricken priest. This view of Assisi is probably the oldest one in existence.

In the side chapel (B) is the crucifix carved by Brother Innocent of Palermo (17th Century).

Above the main altar is a copy of the crucifix which spoke to St. Francis; the original is in Santa Chiara.

In the apse are the stalls, in the center of which is an opening, now covered by the stalls. It was through this opening, once covered by a grill, that the sisters received Communion. It was also through this opening that the Poor Ladies viewed Francis' corpse (see p. 64). The grill was later transported to Santa Chiara.

Through the door on the right of the choir you proceed to the **Sepolcreto**, where the first followers of Clare were buried. Although her sister Agnes and mother Ortolana were once buried here, their bodies were later transferred to a chapel in Santa Chiara.

Through the small door on the left you can look into the sisters' **Choir** (D) where the nuns prayed their Office. The rough-hewn wooden stalls and the rudimentary pulpit speak eloquently of poverty and the prayer of the sisters. The wall with the frescoes dates to the end of the 15th Century. It was added to improve and modernize the choir; however it sealed off access to the Communion grill.

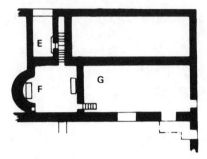

San Damiano (upper story). – E: Garden of St. Clare; – F: Oratory of St. Clare; G: Sisters' Dormitory.

Returning to the **Sepolcreto** and climbing an old stairway, we find the "Garden of St. Clare" (E). It is an extended terrace from which there is a magnificent view of the Spoleto valley. Imagine at the base of the wall the wooden hut where Francis composed the Canticle.

Continuing up the stairs we come to the **Oratory** above the choir of the church. A cupboard contains several relics – the bell which called the sisters to prayer; a small alabaster ostensorium. But the most important and most touching one is the hand-written breviary that Clare and her sisters used to recite the Office. One tradition which, however can only be traced back to the 17th Century says that Brother Leo copied the breviary. However, since well-authenticated samples of Leo's hand-writing are in existence, we can safely say that his was not the professional hand that copied it. Fortunately that does not affect the value of the breviary.

After climbing a few steps, we enter a large, empty rectangular room; this was the sisters' dormitory. On the wall a wooden cross and some flowers near it mark the spot where Clare died on August 11, 1253, saying to herself:

"Depart in security because you have a good guide for the journey; go, because he who created you has also sanctified you; he has always guarded you and kept you in his tender love, as a mother loves her child! May you be blessed, my Lord, who has created me!".

Celano, Vita Santae Chiarae, 46.

We return to the ground level by way of a passage at the far end of the dormitory. Crossing the courtyard we find the refectory. Except for the ceiling which has been redone, nothing has changed here since the time of St. Clare. Here the sisters ate while listening to the Bible. These are the same benches and tables that they used. A small wooden cross still marks the abbess' place. It was also in this refectory that Clare's prayer turned back the Saracens.

Enjoy the flower-filled cloister which was built later; admire the frescoes, especially those in the chapel of St. Jerome (on the right).

SAN FRANCESCO

Francis died on Oct. 3, 1226; the following day he was buried in the church of San Giorgio. Six months later; his counsellor Cardinal Ugolino was elected Pope. Convinced of Francis' sanctity, Pope Gregory IX canonized Francis in San Giorgio on July 16, 1228.

After that, Gregory decided to construct two monuments to St. Francis. The first was a literary one; he commissioned Thomas of Celano to write the life of St. Francis. Finished in 1228, this is what we refer to as the *Vita Prima*.

The second monument was the Basilica of St. Francis. If it was Pope Gregory who brought the basilica to life, it was under the supervision of Brother Elias that it grew. The basilica would be built outside the city walls, on a spot known as "**Collis infernus**" (or more probably **Collis inferiore**); it soon became known as **Collis de Paradiso** because Francis' body was to be transferred there.

Work proceeded well and the construction of the lower basilica was almost finished when, in July of 1230, Francis' remains were transferred there. In 1236 the upper basilica was finished. In 1239 the newly-built campanile had its first bells installed. In 1246 the Commune of Assisi fixed the limits of the upper piazza; since that time any new buildings have been required to preserve the view of the basilica as it was then. Finally, in 1253 the Pope himself came to consecrate the two basilicas.

The terrain itself had some effect on the design of the two superimposed basilicas. First, the nave is oriented toward the west instead of toward the east as is customary Also, the convent was first built towards the west, but then turned back toward the east so as to maintan the view of the piazza. Finally, as it was enlarged it was fortified, especially by the papacy, to which it belongs.

The Basilica of San Francesco is an important place for students of art and architecture. A thorough visit would require several days. However, since the typical pilgrim doesn't have that much time to spend, we will study a few special frescoes.

If you have an hour to spend in the Basilica, follow this program: Go to the basilica by way of Via Frate Elias through the lower piazza; the arcades were built in the 15th century to offer shade to the pilgrims. Along with the basilica, they create an impressive sight.

Enter the lower basilica through the Gothic arched, double arcade (13th century) and carved wooden doors (16th c.); we are entering the basilica by way of the east transept, which was added in the 14th century.

On the left of the entrance is the chapel of **St Sebastian** (A). Cross the transept; at the other end, on the right hand side is the **Chapel of St. Anthony of Egypt** (B). Enter the chapel and turn left into the passageway leading to the old cloister, the ancient cemetery of the friars.

Re-enter the basilica and go to the **second bay of the nave**; from here examine the primitive Italian Gothic style of architecture which retains some romanesque characteristics. Notice the thickness of the main girders and of the pointed arches; without any molding to reinforce them, they sustain the thrust of the vault and of the masssive pillars. The wings of the east transept are covered with a rounded vault.

On the left wall of this bay (D) there are several frescoes attributed to the "Master of St. Francis"; especially noteworthy is the "Sermon to the Birds", which is livelier than Giotto's in the upper basilica.

Taking the stairway on the right, go down to visit the simple tomb of St. Francis. Note, also, the tombs of Leo, Angelo, Masseo, Rufino as well as of Lady Jacoba.

Coming from the crypt, head toward the west transept. Be sure to notice, on the right, the **Madonna with the Angels** (E) by Cimabue. On the extreme right-hand side of this fresco is the famous portrait of St. Francis, corresponding to the verbal portrait by Thomas of Celano:

> He was of medium height, closer to shortness; his head was moderate in size and round, his face a bit long and prominent, his forehead smooth and low; his eyes were of moderate size, black and sound; his hair was black, his eyebrows straight, his nose symmetrical, thin and straight; his ears were upright, but small; his temples smooth. His speech was peaceable, fiery and sharp; his voice was strong, sweet, clear, and sonorous. His teeth were set close together, even, and white; his lips were small and thin; his beard black, but not bushy. His neck was slender, his shoulders straight, his arms short, his hands slender, his fingers long, his nails extended; his legs were thin, his feet small. His skin was delicate, his flesh very spare. He wore rough garments, he slept but very briefly, he gave most generously. And because he was very humble, he showed *all mildness to all men*, adapting himself usefully to the behavior of all. The more holy amongst the holy, among sinners he was as one of them.
>
> *1 Celano, 83.*

As you turn from this fresco, you will find, on the Northwestern corner the entrance to the Chapel of the Relics. Descend into the oldest level of the Sacro Convento to see several special relics, including Francis' hand-written Blessing for Brother Leo.

Going back into the lower basilica, go to the left (southwestern) transept; among the frescoes of Lorenzetti there are three especially noteworthy ones: The Crucifixion (F), the Deposition (G) and the Virgin between St. John and St. Francis.

Climbing one of the stairways along the western wall, we leave the lower church; we find ourselves in the "grand clois-

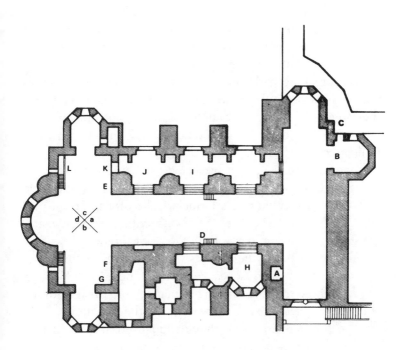

San Francesco (lower basilica). – A: Chapel of Saint Sebastian. – B: Chapel of St. Anthony the abbot. – C: Cloister of the dead. – D: Sermon to the birds. – E: "Madonna of the Angels" by Cimabue. – F and G: Frescoes by Lorenzetti. – H: Chapel of St. Martin. – I: Chapel of St. Anthony of Padua. – J: Chapel of St. Mary Magdalene. – K: "Crucifixion" and "Nativity" by Giotto. – L: "Return to Nazareth"; St. Francis and the Skeleton; a, b, c, d,: the Franciscan allegories.

ter", a two-story courtyard commissioned by the Franciscan Pope Sixtus IV. At the extreme northern end of the courtyard a staircase leads to the upper basilica.

The architectural contrast between the two basilicas is striking, even though they are almost contemporary. The style of the upper church is French Gothic; every beam and every arch ends in a single column crowned with is own distinct capital. Above the Giotto cycle there is a passageway that ends in triple arches in the transept and the apse. However, this French Gothic style is rather awkward and anachronistic. No molding lightens the line of the arches; the large butresses, even though their rose color complements the white rock of the exterior, were not sufficient to counteract the thrust of the vault. In the 14th century they had to add pointed arches. These details among others preclude the design of a French architect; they rather suggest an Italian, possibly a Friar Minor, who was familiar with the churches of France, but did not really know Gothic architecture well.

All the walls of the upper basilica are covered with frescoes. In the nave, the lower register contains the famous Giotto cycle (1295-1300) dedicated to St. Francis. Taken for the most part from the *Legenda Major* of St. Bonaventure these twenty-eight scenes are a summary of the life of St. Francis.

Here are the twenty-eight texts which inspired them. Especially take note of the frescoes we have numbered 4, 5, 6, 7, 13 and 19. In these frescoes Giotto has managed to break with the hierarchical structure and steroetypes of the Byzantine tradition. The portraits are perfectly individualized, but the details of realism have not yet arrived as is evident in Nos. 1, 4, 8, 13 and 23.

1. – A simple man spreads his cloak at Francis' feet:

> His good life, his gentleness and patience, his almost superhuman readiness to oblige, together with his generosity which exceeded his means, and his pleasant manner were so many indications which marked him out as a young man. They seemed to be almost a foretaste of things to come, indicating that the abundance of God's blessings would be heaped upon him more plentifully than ever in the future. Indeed, one citizen of the town, a very simple man who appears to have been inspired by God, took off his cloak when he met Francis in Assisi one day and spread it under his feet, saying that he deserved the respect of everybody because he would do great things and be honored by the whole Church.
>
> *Legenda Major, I, 1.*

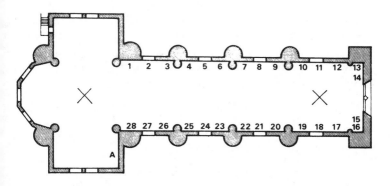

St. Francis (upper basilica). – 1 to 28: Cycle of frescoes by Giotto and his school. – A: "Crucifixion" by Cimabue.

2. – Francis gives his cloak to a poor knight:

When he recovered and was going about dressed as usual in keeping with his position, he met a knight who was of noble birth but very poor, so that he was not properly clad. Francis felt sorry for him and immediately took off his own clothes and gave them to him. At one and the same time he fulfilled the twofold duty of relieving the poverty of the poor and saving a nobleman from embarrassment.

Legenda Major, I, 2.

3. – Francis' dream:

That night as he lay asleep, God in his goodness showed him a vision of a magnificent palace full of armor, bearing Christ's cross as its coat-of-arms. He would let him see that the kindness he had done a poor knight for love of the supreme King would be repaid with an incomparable reward. And so when Francis asked to whom all this belonged, he was told from heaven that it was all for him and his knights.

Legenda Major, I, 3.

4. – Francis hears the voice of the crucifix at San Damiano:

Francis left the town one day to meditate out-of-doors and as he was passing by the church of San Damiano which was threatening to collapse with age, he felt urged to go in and pray. There as he knelt in prayer before a painted image of the Crucified, he felt greatly comforted in spirit and his eyes were full of tears as he gazed at the cross. Then, all of a sudden, he heard a voice coming from the cross and telling him three times, "Francis, go and repair my house. You see it is all falling down".

Legenda Major, II, 1.

5. – Francis renounces his inheritance:

Now that he had recovered his money, he arranged to have Francis brought before the bishop of the diocese, where he should renounce all his claims and return everything he had. In his genuine love for poverty, Francis was more than ready to comply and he willingly appeared before the bishop. There he made no delay – without hesitation, without hearing or saying a word – he immediately took off his clothes and gave them back to his father. Then it was discovered that he wore a hair-shirt under his fine clothes next to his skin. He even took off his trousers in his fervor and enthusiasm and stood there naked before them all. Then he said to his father, "Until now I called you my father, but from now on I can say without reserve. 'Our Father who art in heaven'. He is all my wealth and I place all my confidence in him". When the bishop heard this, he was amazed at his passionate fervor. He jumped to his feet and took Francis into his embrace, covering him with the cloak he was wearing, like the good man that he was. Then he told his servants to bring some clothes for him and they gave him an old tunic which belonged to one of the bishop's farmhands. Francis took it gratefully and drew a cross on it with his own hand with a piece of chalk, making it a worthy garment for a man who was crucified and a beggar. And so the servant of the most high King was left stripped of all that belonged to him, that he might follow the Lord whom he loved, who hung naked on the cross. He was armed with the cross, the means of salvation which would enable him to escape from a shipwrecked world.

Legenda Major, II, 4.

6. – Pope Innoncent's dream:

Only a short time before, he had seen a vision from heaven and by divine inspiration he now testified that it would be fulfilled in Francis. As he himself described it, he had a dream in which he saw the Lateran basilica which was threatening to fall being held up by a poor beggarman who put his back to it. "This is certainly the man", he added. "By his work and teaching, he will uphold Christ's Church".

Legenda Major, III, 10.

7. – The pope approves Francis' way of life:

As a result of his vision the pope was filled with reverence for Francis and granted his request unconditionally. He always had a special regard for him and while granting what he asked, he promised to give the friars greater powers in the future. He approved the rule and gave them a mission to preach repentance, conferring small tonsures on the laymen among Francis' companions, so that they could preach the word of God without interference.

Legenda Major, III, 10.

8. – Francis appears in a fiery chariot:

St. Francis went into Assisi one Saturday because he was to preach as usual in the cathedral the following morning. There he spent the night praying in a shelter in the garden belonging to the canons of the cathedral, as was his custom. In person he was separated from the friars, but then about midnight, as some of them were praying and others slept, a fiery chariot of extraordinary brilliance came in the door of the hut and turned here and there three times about the room. It was surmounted by a globe of light which looked like the sun and lit up the darkness. Those who were awake were dumbfounded, while the others woke up terrified; they could feel the light penetrating their hearts just as it lit up the room, and their consciences were laid bare to one another by force of its brightness. As they read one another's hearts, they all realized simultaneously that their father who was absent from them in person was present with them in spirit under the appearance of this vision. They were sure God had shown him to them in this glorious chariot of fire, radiant with the splendor of heaven and inflamed with burning ardor, so that they might follow him as loyal disciples. Like a second Elias, God had made him a "chariot and charioteer" (cf. 4 Kgs 2: 12) for all spiritual people.

Legenda Major, IV, 4.

9. – An angel shows Brother Pacifico the throne prepared for Francis:

Brother Pacifico was travelling with St. Francis when they went into an abandoned church, where they prayed fervently. There this friar was in an ecstasy and saw a vision of a multitude of thrones in heaven, one of which was radiant with glory and adorned with precious stones and ranked higher than the rest. He marvelled at its splendor and fell to wondering whose it was going to be. Then he heard a voice telling him. "That throne belonged to one of the fallen angels. Now it is being kept for the humble Francis".

Legenda Major, VI, 6.

10. – Francis expels the demons from Arezzo:

On another occasion St. Francis arrived at Arezzo when the whole town was being torn with faction fights and threatened with destruction. There he was given hospitality in a village near the town and he could see the devils rejoicing over it and urging the people on to mutual slaughter. He was anxious to put the malicious powers of evil to flight and so he sent brother Sylvester, who was a man of dove-like simplicity, telling him to approach the town like a herald. "Go up the town gate", he said, "and in the name of almighty God command the devils in virtue of obeiience to go away immediately". Sylvester was a genuinely obedient man and he immediately did what he was told. He approached the town gate, singing a hymn of praise to God, and there he cried aloud, "In the name of almighty God and by the command of his servant Francis, away with you, all you devils!" There and then the town was restored to peace and the townspeople set about reforming the laws governing their mutual rights peacefully.

Legenda Major, VI, 9.

11. – Francis meets the Sultan:

The sultan asked them by whom and why and in what capacity they had been sent, and how they got there; but Francis replied intrepidly that they had been sent by God, not by man, to show him and his subjects the way of salvation and proclaim the truth of the Gospel message. He proclaimed the triune God and Jesus Christ, the Savior of all, with such steadfastness, with such courage and spirit, that it was clear the promise of the Gospel had been fulfilled in him, "I will give you such eloquence and such wisdom as all your adversaries shall not be able to withstand, or to confute" (Lk 21: 15).

When the sultan saw his enthusiasm and courage, he listened to him willingly and pressed him to stay with him. Francis, however, was inspired by God to reply, "If you are willing to become converts to Christ, you and your people, I shall be only too glad to stay with you for love of him. But if you are afraid to abandon the law of Mahomet for Christ's sake, then light a big fire and I will go into it with your priests. That will show you which faith is more sure and more holy". To that the sultan replied, "I do not think that any of my priests would be willing to expose himself to the flames just to defend his faith, or suffer any kind of torture" (he had just caught a glimpse of one of his priests, an old and highly esteemed man, who slipped away the moment he heard Francis' proposal). Then Francis continued, "If you are prepared to promise me that you and your people will embrace the Christian religion, if I come out of the fire unharmed, I will enter it alone. But if I am burned, you must attribute it to my sins; on the other hand, if God saves me by his power, you must acknowledge 'Christ the power of God, Christ the wisdom of God' (cf. I Cor 1: 24) as true God, the Lord and Savior of all". The sultan replied that he would not dare to accept a choice like that, for fear of a revolt among his people.

Then he offered Francis a number of valuable presents, but the saint was anxious only for the salvation of souls; he had no interest in the things of this earth and so he scorned them all as if they were so much dust. The sultan was lost in admiration at the sight of such perfect disregard for worldly wealth and he felt greater respect than ever for the saint. He refused, or perhaps did not dare, to become a Christian, but at the same time he implored the saint to take the gifts and give them to the Christian poor or to churches, for his salvation. Francis, however. did not want to be bothered with money and besides he could see no sign of a genuinely religious spirit in the sultan, and so he absolutely refused to agree.

Legenda Major, IX, 8.

12. – Francis in ecstasy:

One night he was seen deep in prayer, his hands stretched out in the form of a cross. The brilliance which enveloped his body was a sign of the miraculous light which flooded his soul.

Legenda Major, X, 4.

13. – Christmas at Greccio.

Three years before he died St. Francis decided to celebrate the memory of the birth of the Child Jesus at Greccio, with the greatest possible solemnity. He asked and obtained the permission of the pope for the ceremony, so that he could not be accused of being an innovator, and then he had a crib prepared, with hay and an ox and an ass. The friars were all invited and the people came in crowds. The forest re-echoed with their voices and the night was lit up with a multitude of bright lights, while the beautiful music of God's praises added to the solemnity. The saint stood before the crib and his heart overflowed with tender compassion; he was bathed in tears but overcome with joy. The Mass was sung there and Francis, who was a deacon, sang the Gospel. Then he preached to the people about the birth of the poor King, whom he called the Babe of Bethlehem in his tender love.

A knight called John from Greccio, a pious and truthful man who had abandoned his profession in the world for love of Christ and was a great friend of St. Francis, claimed that he saw a beautiful child asleep in the crib, and that St. Francis took it in his arms and seemed to wake it up.

The integrity of this witness and the miracles which afterwards took place, as well as the truth indicated by the vision itself, all go to prove its reality. The example which Francis put before the world was calculated to rouse the hearts of those who are weak in the faith, and the hay from the crib, which was kept by the people, afterwards cured sick animals and drove off various pestilences. Thus God wished to give glory to his servant Francis and prove the efficacy of his prayers by clear signs.

Legenda Major, X, 7.

14. – The miraculous fountain:

Another time, while travelling to a hermitage where he planned to devote himself to prayer, St. Francis rode an ass belonging to a poor laborer because he was weak. It was summertime and, as the owner of the animal followed the saint into the mountains, he was exhausted by the long and gruelling journey. Fainting with thirst, he suddenly cried out after the saint. "I'll die of thirst, if I don't get a drink immediately". Francis dismounted there and then and knelt on the ground with his hands stretched out to heaven, and there he prayed until he knew that he had been heard. When he had finished, he told his benefactor, "Go to that rock and you will find running water. Christ in his mercy had made it flow there for you just now". By God's wonderful condescension which bows so easily to his servants a thirsty human being was able to drink from a rock, quenching his thirst from solid stone, by the power of one man's prayer. Water had never been found at that spot before and none could ever be found there afterwards, although a careful search was made.

Legenda Major, VII, 12.

15. – The sermon to the birds:

When he was near Bevagna, he came to a spot where there was a huge flock of birds of various kinds. The moment he saw them, he ran to them and greeted them as if they unterstood, and they all turned towards him and waited for him. Those that had perched on the bushes bent their heads, when he came near, and looked at him in an extraordinary way. He went straight up to them and appealed to them all to hear the word of God saying. "My brothers, you have a great obligation to praise your Creator. He clothed you with feathers and gave you wings to fly, appointing the clear air as your home, and he looks after you without any effort on your part". As he continued speaking to them like this, the birds showed their pleasure in a wonderful fashion; they stretched our their necks and flapped their wings, gazing at him with their beaks open. In his spiritual enthusiasm Francis walked among them, brushing them with his habit, and not one of them moved until he made the sign of the cross and gave them permission to go. Then they all flew away together with his blessing. His companions who were waiting on the road saw everything and when the saint rejoined them, in the purity and simplicity of his heart, he began to reproach himself for his negligence in never preaching to the birds before.

Legenda Major, XII, 3.

16. – Francis predicts the death of the knight of Celano:

Another time, after his return from overseas, St. Francis went to preach at Celano and a knight begged him to come and have dinner with him. So he came to the house and the whole family was there to celebrate his arrival with his companions. However, before they sat down St. Francis offered praise to God, as was his custom, and stood there praying, with his eyes raised to heaven. When he had finished, he beckoned his generous host aside and told him, "Brother host, you persuaded me to come and dine with you, and I came. But now do what I tell you immediately, because you are going to eat in another world, not here on this earth. Confess all your sins with genuine sorrow and leave nothing untold. God means to reward you today for having given his poor such a warm welcome". The knight took his advice and confessed all his sins to Francis' companion, and put his affairs in order, doing everything he could to prepare for death. Eventually they took their places at table and just as they were beginning to eat, their host suddenly dropped dead, as the saint had foretold. So it was that as a reward for his kindness in showing hospitality, he received the reward given to prophets, because he had given a prophet the welcome due to a prophet, as we read in the Gospel (cf. Mt 10: 41). Warned by the saint's prophecy, the knight had prepared for immediate death and clad in the armor of repentance he escaped eternal damnation and was received into the eternal dwelling places.

Legenda Major, XI, 4.

17. – Francis preaches to the pope:

Francis' words were like a blazing fire which penetrated the depths of the heart and filled the minds of his hearers with wonder. They had no claim to any literary style, but gave every sign of being the result of divine inspiration.

He was due to preach before the pope and the cardinals on one occasion and at the suggestion of the bishop of Ostia he learned a carefully prepared sermon by heart. But when he stood before them all to deliver his edifying message, his mind went blank and he could not remember a word. He told them what had happened quite humbly and invoked the aid of the Holy Spirit. Then his tongue was suddenly unloosed and he spoke so eloquently that he moved the hearts of his exalted listeners to true sorrow, and it was clear that it was the Spirit of God who spoke, not he.

Legenda Major, XII, 7.

18. – Francis appears at the Chapter of Arles:

Francis could not preside personally at the chapter of the different provinces, but by his unremitting prayer and the power of his blessing he was always there in spirit in his anxious care for his subjects. On one occasion he even appeared visibly at such a chapter by God's power. It was at the chapter of Arles and the famous preacher whom we now honor as St. Anthony was preaching to the friars on the proclamation Pilate wrote on the Cross, "Jesus of Nazareth, the king of the Jews". One of the friars, a holy man named Monaldus, felt a sudden inspiration to look towards the door of the chapter hall; there with his own eyes, he saw St. Francis standing in mid-air with his arms stretched out in the form of a cross, blessing the friars.

Legenda Major, IV, 10.

19. – Francis receives the stigmata:

The fervor of his seraphic longing raised Francis up to God and, in an ecstasy of compassion, made him like Christ who allowed himself to be crucified in the excess of his love. Then one morning about the feast of the Exaltation of the Holy Cross, while he was praying on the mountainside, Francis saw a Seraph with six fiery wings coming down from the highest point in the heavens. The vision descended swiftly and came to rest in the air near him. Then he saw the image of a Man crucified in the midst of the wings, with his hands and feet stretched out and nailed to a cross. Two of the wings were raised above his head and two were stretched out in flight, while the remaining two shielded his body. Francis was dumbfounded at the sight and his heart was flooded with a mixture of joy and sorrow. He was overjoyed at the way Christ regarded him so graciously under the appearance of a Seraph, but the fact that he was nailed to a cross pierced his soul with a sword of compassionate sorrow.

He was lost in wonder at the sight of this mysterious vision; he knew that the agony of Christ's passion was not in keeping with the state of a seraphic spirit which is immortal. Eventually he realized by divine inspiration that God has shown him this vision in his providence, in order to let him see that, as Christ's lover, he would resemble Christ crucified perfectly not by physical martyrdom, but by the fervor of his spirit. As the vision disappeared, it left his heart ablaze with eagerness and impressed upon his body a miraculous likeness. There and then the marks of nails began to appear in his hands and feet, just as he had seen them in his vision of the Man nailed to the Cross. His hands and feet appeared pierced through the center with nails, the heads of which were in the palms of his hands and on the instep of each foot, while the points stuck out on the opposite side. The heads were black and round, but the points were long and bent back, as if they had been struck with a hammer; they rose above the surrounding flesh and stood out from it. His right side seemed as if it had been pierced with a lance and was marked with a livid scar which often bled, so that his habit and trousers were stained.

Legenda Major, XII, 3.

20. – The death and funeral of St. Francis:

At last, when all God's mysteries had been accomplished in him, his holy soul was freed from his body and assumed into the abyss of God's glory, and Francis fell asleep in God. One of the friars, a disciple of his, saw his soul being borne on a white cloud over many waters to heaven, under the appearance of a radiant star. It shone with the brightness of sublime sanctity, full of the abundance of divine wisdom and grace which had earned for him the right to enter the home of light and peace, where he rests with Christ for ever.

Legenda Major, XIV, 6.

21. – The visions of Brother Augustine and the bishop of Assisi:

The provincial minister of the friars in the Terra di Lavoro, Brother Augustine, a holy and upright man, was at death's door at that time. He had been unable to speak for some time, but now those who were with him suddenly heard him crying out, "Wait for me, father. Wait! I am coming with you". The friars were amazed and asked him to whom he was speaking. He replied, "Can't you see our father Francis. He is going to heaven". There and then his holy soul left his body and followed his father.

The bishop of Assisi was on a pilgrimage to the shrine of St. Michael on Monte Gargano at that time, and St. Francis appeared to him on the night of his death, saying, "See, I am leaving the world and going to heaven". When he got up in the morning, the bishop told his companions what had happened. On his return to Assisi, he investigated the matter carefully and came to the conclusion that St. Francis left the world at the time he appeared to him in his vision.

At the time of St. Francis' death, when it was already dusk, a great flock of larks gathered over the building, although they normally prefer the light of day and avoid the shades of night. There they remained, flying about and singing with unusual joy, clearly testifying by the sweetness of their song to the glory of the saint who had so often called upon them to praise God.

Legenda Major, XIV, 6.

22. – The knight, Jerome, is assured of the reality of the stigmata

One of those who was allowed to see the body of St. Francis was a knight called Jerome who was an educated and prudent man. He was a very well known person, but he was unbelieving like the Apostle St. Thomas and he doubted the reality of the stigmata. In his eagerness he did not hesitate to move the nails in full sight of the friars and all the people, and he felt the saint's hands and feet and side with his fingers. As he felt the marks of Christ's wounds under his touch, the doubt vanished from his heart and from the hearts of others. As a result he and many others afterwards bore witness to the truth which he had verified so carefully, and swore to it on the Gospel.

Legenda Major, XV, 4.

23. – The Clares mourn Francis:

Francis' friars and sons who had been summoned to his deathbed spent the night on which he died singing God's praises with all the people, so that it seemed as if angels were keeping watch and no one would think obsequies were being celebrated for the dead. In the morning the crowd which had gathered took branches from the trees and brought his body to Assisi, singing hymns and canticles and carriyng a multitude of lights. As they passed the church of San Damiano where the noble Virgin Clare who is now in glory in heaven lived with her sisters, they made a short stop and let them see and kiss his body with its heavenly jewels.

Legenda Major, XV, 5.

24. – The canonization of St. Francis.

The pope was fully convinced of his extraordinary sanctity, not only by the miracles which he heard about after his death, but also by what he knew from his own experience during the saint's lifetime, what he had seen with his own eyes and touched with his own hands. He had no doubt whatever that Francis had already been glorified by God in heaven and in his anxiety to act in harmony with Christ whose Vicar he was, he was disposed to glorify him on earth, as being worthy of all veneration. He had the various miracles worked by the saint recorded in writing and approved by witnesses, in order to convince the whole world that Francis had been glorified in heaven. Then he submitted them to be examined by the cardinals who seemed to be least favorable to the process and when they had checked them carefully and agreed unanimously, he decreed that Francis should be canonized, with the advice and consent of the cardinals and of all the prelates who were then in the papal court. On Sunday, July 16, in the year of our Lord 1228, the pope himself came to Assisi and canonized St. Francis in a long ceremony which it would be tedious to describe.

Legenda Major, XV, 7.

25. – St. Francis appears to Pope Gregory IX:

His Holiness Pope Gregory IX of happy memory, of whom St. Francis had foretold that he would be pope, was inclined to doubt the wound in Francis' side, before the canonization of the saint. Then one night, as the pope himself used to relate with tears, St. Francis appeared to him in a dream. His face seemed a little hard and he reproached him for his doubts. Then he raised his right arm and showed him the wound and told him to get a glass and catch the blood which was streaming from his side. The pope got the glass in his vision and it seemed to fill up to the brim with blood. After that, he was so devoted to the stigmata and so eager in his conviction that he could never allow anyone to call these wonderful signs into doubt by attacking them in their pride, and he corrected such people severely.

Legenda Major, Miracles I, 2.

26. – St. Francis cures a man:

At Lerida a man named John, who had great devotion to St. Francis, was wounded so badly one night that no one could believe he would survive the night. Then St. Francis appeared to him in a vision and touched his wounds with his sacred hands. There and then he restored him to perfect health, so that the whole countryside was loud in its praise of the standard-bearer of the Cross, saying that he was worthy of everyone's veneration. Who would not be surprised to see an acquaintance of his cruelly injured and then enjoying perfect health, at almost one and the same time? Who could remember that without being moved to give thanks? Certainly, no one could recall such a miracle of power and goodness in a spirit of faith, without feeling some increase of devotion.

Legenda minor, VI, 7.

27. – St. Francis restores a woman to life:

At Monte Marano near Benevento, a woman who was noble by birth and still more noble because of her virtue, had a special devotion to St. Francis and honored him reverently and devoutly. She became ill, her condition worsened and she finally "went the way of all flesh". Since her death occurred in the evening, her funeral was delayed until the next day to permit her many relatives and friends to come. The clergy assembled in her home that night to pray the nocturn for the dead and all around there were many men and women praying.

Suddenly before the eyes of the whole crowd, the woman rose from her bed and called to one of the priests, who had been her pastor, saying, "I want to confess my sins, father; please hear my confession. I am dead, and I would have to endure the most difficult punishment because of a sin I failed to confess. But, St. Francis, for whom I have always had great devotion, interceded for me and I was granted permission to return to my body, confess my sins and receive absolution. You will all see, after that I will enter the eternal rest which I have been promised". And, trembling, she made her confession to the priest who was trembling even more. She received absolution, lay back down and fell asleep happily in the Lord.

Celano, Tract. de Mirac. 40.

28. – Peter of Alife is rescued from prison:

During the reign of the Lord Pope Gregory IX it became necessary to undertake a crusade against the heretics in various countries. A certain Peter of Alife, suspected of heresy, was captured in Rome in the company of members of a heretical sect. The Lord Pope Gregory handed him over to the custody of the Bishop of Tivoli who, having received him under pain of losing his diocese, placed the prisoner in irons.

The prisoner's simplicity, however, was a witness to his innocence, and the guards relaxed their harshness. Several noblemen of the city, who had hated the bishop for a very long time, would have been very happy to see him subject to the penalty with which the Pope had threatened him. They secretly advised Peter to escape; the prisoner listened to them and, escaping one night, fled far away.

When the escape was discovered, the bishop was very upset because he feared the punishment which he would receive because of the success of his enemies' plans. He began to pursue the man and sent emissaries in every direction; they succeeded in capturing the poor man, reproached him for his ingratitude and put him under tighter security. He was placed in a dark cell with thick walls, which were reinforced with wooden boards joined with iron nails. They put him in iron chains weighing several pounds and gave him limited amounts of food and drink.

He had given up all hope of ever being free, but God did not want the innocent man to perish and in his mercy He came to his aid. The poor man began, with many tears, to call upon the blessed Francis to have pity on him, because it was the vigil of his feast. This man had great faith in St. Francis because, he said, the heretics often preached against him. And as evening fell, the saint, moved with compassion, went into the prison, called the man by name and ordered him to get up without delay.

– "Who are you?" he asked, astonished.

– "St. Francis" he heard the reply.

He called a guard and said to him, "I'm afraid. There's someone here pretending to be St. Francis and he ordered me to get up and leave".

– "Calm down, you poor man! Go to bed and sleep", the guard said. "You're hallucinating because you did not eat enough today".

The saint returned around noon; he repeated his command to get up and the prisoner saw the chains he wore fall one by one to the ground about his feet. The pieces of wood which had reinforced his cell came off the wall and fell together in a heap; the path to freedom lay open before him. Restrained now only by his fear, he could not flee. He went to the door and his cries so frightened the guards that they went to the bishop, saying, "The prisoner has broken his chains". The bishop, still unaware of the miracle which had taken place, thought that he had escaped and, overcome, fell into a faint into his armchair. Then, when he learned all of the details, he went to the prison with great devotion and, recognizing the signs of God's power, worshipped the Lord in that place.

They took the remains of the chains to the Lord Pope and his cardinals; they all marvelled at the sight and blessed the Lord.

Celano, Tract. de Mirac., 93.

After viewing the frescoes by Giotto, leave the basilica by way of the main door; stop to admire the facade and the rose window.

If you have more time to spend, for example a half day, make a more thorough visit to the basilica. In addition to the items listed above, you will have time to notice:

In the lower basilica

1. The frescoes of Simone Martini in the **chapel of St. Martin** (H). There is a machine that will explain them for a modest fee.

2. The stained-glass windows in the chapel of **St. Anthony** (I).

3. The Giotto frescoes in the **chapel of the Magdalene** (J).

4. The four frescoes on the vault over the main altar, representing Poverty (a), Obedience (b), Chastity (c), and the triumph of St. Francis (d).

5. On the right transept among the Giotto frescoes of the life of Christ, notice the **Crucifixion** (K) (beside the Madonna and the Angels) and the **Nativity** beneath it.

On the opposite (western) side above and to the right of the exit there is a "Return to Nazareth" (L) wich is noteworthy for its depiction of Jerusalem. Above, and at the extreme corner of the stairway is **St. Francis with a skeleton wearing a crown**. Perhaps this is a reference to the following text:

> Another time, sitting with his companions, the blessed Francis spoke something like this with a deep sigh: "There is hardly a religious in the whole world who obeys his superior perfectly". Greatly moved, his companions said to him: "Tell us, Father, what is the perfect and highest obedience". And he replied, describing the truly obedient man under the figure of a dead body: "Take a lifeless body and place it where you will. You will see that it does not resist being moved it does not murmur about its position, it does not cry out if it is allowed to lie there. If it is placed on a chair, it will not look up but down; if it is clothed in purple, it looks twice as pale. This", he said, "is a truly obedient man; he does not ask why he is moved, he cares not where he is placed, he does not insist on being changed elsewhere. Raised to an office, he retains his accustomed humility; the more he is honored, the more unworthy does he consider himself".
>
> *2 Celano, 152.*

In the upper basilica

1. In the **left transept** (A) Cimabue's large "Crucifixion"; the use of a lead-based paint which has deteriorated has given this fresco the appearance of a photographic negative.

2. In the **apse** and **transepts**, a remarkable set of **carved choir stalls** decorated with inlaid patterns (1491-1501). The ones in the transept are especially interesting with their optical illusions which are astonishingly modern and almost surrealistic.

3. On the **vault of the transept** are the **four Evangelists** by Cimabue.

4. In the **nave**, the upper and middle registers on the northern side are scenes from the Old Testament; on the southern wall is the New Testament. In general these scenes are in a bad state and their artists cannot be determined. However, we should notice: **The Creation of the World** (upper register, 1); **Noah bullds the Ark** (middle register, 2); **The Sacrifice of Abraham** (middle register, 4); **Esau and Isaac** (middle register, 9); **Joseph forgives his brothers** (middle register, 12); **Judas' kiss** (middle register, 25); and the **Nativity** (upper register, 25).

5. On the vault of **the first bay of the nave**, the **Four Doctors** of the Church by Giotto or one of his disciples.

SAN NICOLO

At the corner of the **Piazza del Comune** (where the Post Office now stands) the church of San Nicolo once stood. All that is left today is the crypt. The entrance is at No. 2 **Via Portica**.

Consulting the Gospel

After Bernardo di Quintavalle told Francis of his desire to follow Christ, the two of them went to confirm their Gospel desire:

> Therefore, they rose early; and with another man named Peter, who also wished to join them, they went to the church of Saint Nicholas near the chief square of the city. They went in to pray, but, being

simple men, they did not know how to find the passage in the Gospel telling of the renunciation of the world. Therefore, they besought God that he would show them his will the first time they opened the book. When their prayer was ended, blessed Francis, kneeling before the altar, took the closed book, opened it and saw written: "If you wish to be perfect, go, sell what you have, and give to the poor, and you shall have treasure in heaven" (Mt. 19: 21). At this blessed Francis gave thanks to God whith great joy; but because of his devotion to the blessed Trinity, he desired a threefold confirmation of the words and opened the book of the Gospel a second and a third time. At the second opening he read: "Take nothing for your journey" (Lk. 9: 3), and at the third: "If any man will come after me, let him deny himself" (Mt. 16: 24). Each time he opened the book blessed Francis gave thanks to God for this threefold confirmation of the resolution and desire which he had long held in his heart; and he said to the aforementioned Bernard and Peter: "O Brothers, this is our life and rule and the life and rule of all those who may wish to join us. Go, therefore, and act on what you have heard".

So Master Bernard, who was very rich, sold all his possessions, and distributed a great deal of money to the poor of the city. Peter too, according to his means, followed our Lord's counsel. Having sold everything, these two both took the habit of poverty which blessed Francis had already adopted when he abandoned the life of a hermit; and from then on, he and they lived according to the precept of the holy Gospel as the Lord had shown them. Because of this blessed Francis said in his *Testament*: "The Lord himself showed me that I should live according to the holy Gospel".

Legend of the Three Companions, 28-29.

SAN RUFINO

The Cathedral of Assisi was begun in 1140; construction continued until the second third of the 13th century. The facade is an excellent example of Romanesque architecture. Completely renovated in the 16th century by Galeazzo Alessi, the interior contrasts sharply with the austere beauty of the facade. We can only regret the disappearance of the romanesque interior which Francis knew.

There are a number of Franciscan stories associated with this church and its surrounding area:

The baptism of Francis

Although this cathedral was not completed at the time of the birth of Francis, he was probably baptized here. Nonetheless, the baptismal font, located to the right as you enter the church, is the one where both Francis and Clare became children of God:

> Francis, the servant and friend of the Most High, to whom divine providence gave this name so that by means of this singular and unusual name the knowledge of his ministry might be known to the whole world, was called John by his mother, when, being born again

of water and the Holy Spirit, he was made a child of grace from a child of wrath.

2 Celano, 3.

His mother wished the child to be called John, but when his father returned from France, he insisted that his son should be called Francis after the country he had recently left.

Legend of the Three Companions, 3.

The fiery chariot

Near the sacristy you can visit the grotto where Francis would go to pray when he came to preach in the cathedral. One time, as he was spending the night there his brothers at Rivo Torto had a mysterious vision:

> Walking in simplicity before God and in confidence before men, the brothers merited at this time to be filled with gladness by means of a divine revelation. For while, kindled by the fire of the Holy Spirit, they chanted the *Pater Noster*, not only at the appointed hours, but at all hours, with supplicant and melodious voice, being little occupied with earthly solicitude and troublesome anxiety of cares, the most blessed father Francis absented himself one night from them in body. And behold, about midnight, when some of the brothers were resting and some were praying in silence with great devotion, a most splendid fiery chariot entered through the door of the house and turned around two or three times here and there inside the house; a huge globe of light rested above it, much like the sun, and it lit up the night. The watchers were dazed and those who had been asleep were frightened; and they felt no less a lighting up of the heart than a lighting up of the body. Gathering together, they, began to ask one another what it was; but by the strength and grace of that great light each one's conscience was revealed to the others. Finally they understood and knew that it was the soul of their holy father that was shining with such great brilliance and that, on account of the grace of his understanding purity and his great tenderness for his sons, he merited to receive such a blessing from God.

1 Celano, 47.

St. Clare

Nothing remains of Clare's family home, but its location is known thanks to a notarized document of 1148 in which Clare's grandfather promises not to enlarge his house to the point that it would ruin the harmony with the new cathedral. From this house, which was located on the piazza, on the lefthand side, Clare was taken to the baptismal font; from it she left to follow Christ on Palm Sunday, 1212. The cathedral was the scene of a dramatic event of great significance:

> Palm Sunday was near and Clare came to see Francis, asking him again what she should do and how she should flee the world. The holy Father ordered her to put on her best clothes and join the rest of the people in the procession. Then, in the following night, she should leave the city and forsake the joys of this world in order to join in the Passion of Christ. When Sunday came the maiden, radiant in her finery, joined the other women of Assisi and entered the church. But something strange took place, which may be seen as an omen. When all of the participants went to receive the blessed palms, Clare, overcome with timidity, stayed in her place. But the celebrant descended from the sanctuary, approached her and placed the palm in her hands.
>
> That night she made all the preparations as the saint had told her and, followed by a devout company, finally made the exit she had so ardently desired.
>
> Since she did not want to go out by the usual door, she chose instead an exit which had been covered over with branches and stones; these she removed with her own hands, displaying an astonishing courage.
>
> *Celano, Vita S. Chiara, 7.*

Brother Sylvester

Sylvester was a canon of San Rufino when, in 1209 or 1210, he left to join Francis. He was the first priest to enter the Order. Although he lived for many years at the Carceri, it is at San Rufino that we can contemplate his conversion. The scene begins when Bernard of Quintavalle is giving his goods to the poor:

A priest named Sylvester was also present from whom Francis had bought some stones when he was repairing the church of Saint Damian and was still alone without any companions. Seeing so much money being scattered about on Francis' advice, Sylvester was moved by envy and approached the servant of God, saying: "You did not fully pay for those stones you bought from me".

Francis scorned avarice and greed, and when he heard this unjust complaint, he went up to Bernard, and putting his hand into the pocket of Bernard's cloak which contained the money, he drew out a handful of coins, and in great fervor of spirit gave them to the dissatisfied priest, saying: "Are you fully paid now, Master Priest?" Sylvester replied, "Yes, Brother", and went home, well pleased with what he had received.

But a few days later, by divine inspiration, this same priest began to reflect on Francis' action, and said to himself: "Am I not a miserable man, old as I am, to be avid for temporal goods, when this young man despises and hates them for love of God?" During the following night in a dream he saw an immense cross reaching to the sky, and its foot was planted in the mouth of Francis, while the arms spread from one end of the world to the other. On awaking, the priest realized and was convinced that blessed Francis was indeed the friend and servant of Jesus Christ and that the form of religion he was introducing would spread over the entire earth. Thus Sylvester was brought to fear God, and he began to do penance while still living in his own house. Before long, however, he entered the fraternity in which he lived perfectly and died gloriously.

Legend of the Three Companions, 30-31.

Brother Rufino

Rufino was the cousin of St. Clare. He joined the group around 1210 when the first friars returned from Rome with the pope's approval of their way of life. A modest man, Rufino became a great contemplative. Although the Fioretti doesn't tell us that this event took place in the cathedral, we can take this opportunity to reflect on the preaching style of Francis and the first friars.

Brother Rufino was so absorbed in God as a result of continual contemplation that he became almost mute and insensible to external things. He used to speak very rarely, and, besides, he had neither the gift nor courage nor ability to preach the word of God.

Nevertheless, one day St. Francis told Brother Rufino to go to Assisi and preach to the people whatever God would inspire him to say.

But Brother Rufino answered: "Reverend Father, please excuse me and don't send me on that assignment because, as you well know, I do not have the grace of preaching, and also I am just a simple ignorant fellow".

Then St. Francis said: "Because you did not obey me at once. I also command you under holy obedience to go to Assisi naked wearing only your breeches – and to go into some church and preach to the people naked like that!".

At this command Brother Rufino obediently undressed and went to Assisi naked and entered into a church. And after he had knelt in reverence before the altar, he went up into the pulpit and began to preach.

At this, the children and men began to laugh and to say: "Look – they are doing so much penance they have gone crazy!".

Meanwhile, St. Francis, thinking over the prompt obedience of Brother Rufino, who was one of the foremost gentlemen of Assisi, and the very difficult command he had given him, began to reproach himself very severely, saying: "How can you, the son of Peter Bernardone – you vile little wretch – order Brother Rufino, who is one of the noblest citizens of Assisi, to go naked and preach to the people like a madman? By God, I am going to see to it that you yourself experience what you order others to do!".

And having said that, in the fervor of the Holy Spirit he too immediately took off his habit and went to Assisi naked, accompanied by Brother Leo, who very discreetly carried along the Saint's habit and Brother Rufino's.

And when the people of Assisi saw him naked too, they laughed at him as at a lunatic, thinking that both he and Brother Rufino had gone mad from doing too much penance.

But St. Francis found and entered the church where Brother Rufino had already begun to preach. And he was saying these words devoutly and severely: "Oh, dear people, flee the world. Give up sin. Restore to others what belongs to them if you want to escape hell. But keep God's commandments and love God and your neighbor if you want to go to Heaven. And do penance, because the Kingdom of Heaven is drawing near!".

Then St. Francis went up naked into the pulpit, and he began to preach so marvelously about contempt of the world, holy penance, holy voluntary poverty, the desire for the Kingdom of Heaven, and about the nakedness and humiliations and most holy Passion of Our Lord Jesus Crucified that the whole crowd of men and women who had gathered there for the sermon in great numbers began to weep very bitterly. And with unbelievable devotion and compunction of heart they cried out aloud to God for mercy, so that nearly all of them were converted to a new state of mind.

And not only there, but throughout all Assisi on that day there was such mourning among the people over the Passion of Our Lord Jesus Christ that so much weeping had never been heard in that town.

And after the people had thus been edified and Christ's sheep had been consoled by the deed of St. Francis and Brother Rufino, and after they had received a blessing in the name of Our Lord Jesus Christ, St. Francis put Brother Rufino's habit on him again, and he himself got dressed with him.

And so wearing their habits once more, they went back to the place of the Portiuncola, glorifying and praising the Lord for having given them the grace to overcome themselves by self-contempt and for having edified the little sheep of Christ by their good example and for having shown how the world is to be despised.

And on that day the devotion of the people toward them increased so much that those who could touch the hem of their clothes considered themselves blessed.

To the glory of Our Lord Jesus Christ, who is blessed! Amen.

Fioretti, 30.

SANTA CHIARA

The basilica of Santa Chiara, begun in 1257 and consecrated in 1265 is a smaller replica of the upper church of San Francesco. On the exterior, the "flying buttresses" added at the end of the 14th century add a bit of architectural charm and a touch of strength to this easily identifiable church.

The basilica was built on the site of the church of San Giorgio, which was located outside of the city walls. It was in this

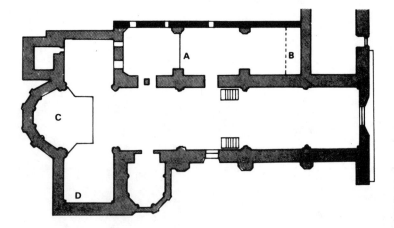

Santa Chiara. – Black: the remains of San Giorgio. – A: Crucifix of San Damiano. – B: Relics. – C: The large Crucifix. – D: The Nativity.

church that the young Francis learned to read; it was here also that his body lay from 1226 to 1230. This church also witnessed the canonization of Francis by Gregory IX in 1228. And it was in San Giorgio that Clare's remains were kept until the basilica became a reality.

Of the Church of San Giorgio, probably only the southern wall remains; the visitor should head there first, for on the glass wall which closes in the Blessed Sacrament chapel, we find the crucifix of San Damiano (A) which spoke to Francis in 1205. In front of this crucifix, Francis prayed:

> Most high,
> glorious God,
> enlighten the darkness of my heart
> and give me, Lord,
> a correct faith,
> a certain hope,
> a perfect charity,
> sense and knowledge,
> so that I may carry out Your holy and true command.

In the rear of this chapel there are some remarkable relics. Of particular significance is the breviary which Francis and his brothers used to recite the Office. On the front page, Brother Leo wrote the following:

> "Blessed Francis obtained this breviary for his companions, Brother Angelo and Brother Leo, and he always wanted to use it to say the Office when his health permitted, as is prescribed in the Rule. Sickness prevented him from saying the Office, but he at least wanted to listen to it. His whole life long, he was faithful to that.
>
> He also had this Book of the Gospels copied and when sickness or anything else prevented him from attending Mass he would have the Gospel of the day read to him. He was also faithful to this until he died. He used to say: When I cannot attend Mass, I adore the body of Christ with the eyes of my soul in my prayer just as I adore It when I see It at Mass. Whenever he finished reading or hearing the Gospel, Francis would kiss the text as a sign of respect for the Lord.
>
> That is why Brothers Angelo and Leo ask the Lady Benedetta, abbess of the Poor Ladies of the Monastery of Santa Chiara and all the

future abbesses, as much as they can, to always preserve this breviary in the monastery of Santa Chiara in remembrance of our holy Father and out of devotion to him who so often read from it.

In the crypt there is the body of St. Clare discovered in 1850. Climb the all stairway in the center of the crypt to see the stone coffin in which Clare's body lay for almost 600 years.

Returning to the church you will notice the large 13th-century crucifix (C) over the main altar; in the left transept there is a small miracle; a fragment of a 14th-century fresco of the nativity (D). In addition to that, there are numerous fragments of frescoes, all that remain of a decoration which was once as abundant as that of San Francesco.

STREETS
and
PIAZZAS

The best way to discover any city is by strolling aimlessly along the streets; Assisi is no exception. Basically it consists of a number of streets that meet in the **Piazza del Comune**; these are connected to one another by many picturesque side streets, many of them hardly more than stairways. By taking these side-streets you can capture some of the medieval charm of the city; you might even meet St. Francis there. As a child he certainly played here; as a young man he and his friends probably came along these streets to serenade a pretty girl or to play a trick on some citizens. After his conversion, he often walked these streets, at first scorned and harassed by his fellow citizens, later admired and followed by them. But, as he walked these streets, he was united with Christ.

The King of youth

The young people of Assisi had formed a group that met together to eat, drink and sing. Francis was a member and several times he was chosen leader. But, grace was at work in him and he began to acquire different tastes:

Soon after Francis had returned to Assisi, his companions elected him king of the revels, and gave him a free hand to spend what he liked in the preparation of a sumptuous banquet as he had often done on other occasions. After the feast they left the house and started off singing through the streets. Francis' companions were leading the way; and he holding his wand of office, followed them at a little distance. Instead of singing, he was listening very attentively. All of a sudden the Lord touched his heart, filling it with such surpassing sweetness that he could neither speak nor move. He could only feel and hear this overwhelming sweetness which detached him so completely from all other physical sensations that, as he said later, had he been cut to pieces on the spot he could not have moved.

When his companions looked around, they saw him in the distance and turned back. To their amazement they saw that he was transformed into another man, and they asked asked him: "What were you thinking of? Why didn't you follow us? Were you thinking of getting married?"

Francis answered in a clear voice: "You are right: I was thinking of wooing the noblest, richest, and most beautiful bride ever seen". His friends laughed at him saying he was a fool and did not know what he was saying; in reality he had spoken by a divine inspiration. The bride was none other than that form of true religion which he embraced; and which, above any other is noble, rich, and beautiful by its poverty. From that hour he began to consider himself as naught and to despise all those things he had formerly cherished; but he still did so imperfectly, not being as yet entirely detached from worldly vanities. He gradually withdrew from the tumult of earthly things and applied himself secretly to receive Jesus Christ into his soul with that pearl of great price which he so desired as to be willing to sell all he possessed in order to gain it. To this end he often hid himself from the eyes of deceitful men and withdrew to pray in secret, incited to do so by the same sweetness in his heart which took possession of him with increasing frequency, drawing him apart to pray far from all public meeting places.

He was already a benefactor of the poor, but from this time onwards he resolved never to refuse alms to anyone who begged in God's name; but rather to give more willingly and abundantly than ever before. If a poor person begged of him when he was far from home, he would always give him money, if possible; when he had none he would give his belt or buckle; or, if he had not even these, he would find a hiding place and, taking off his shirt, give it to the beggar for love of God. In addition to this, he was most liberal in buying vases and other objects pertaining to the service and adornment of churches and he sent them secretly to poor priests.

Legend of the Three Companions, 7-8.

Stones to repair San Damiano

At San Damiano Francis had heard the Crucifix speak to him: "Go and repair my house which is falling into ruins". The chapel really was in ruins; the command seemed quite simple. But the priest refused to take the money which Francis offered him. Since there was no other way, he had to beg for stones, because it would take many of them to restore the little church:

> Then he started back to the city where he began to praise God loudly in the streets and public places; and when he had finished his song of praise, he set to begging for stones with which to restore the church. He called to the passers-by: "Whoever gives me one stone will have one reward, two stones, two rewards; three stones, a treble reward". Many other simple words fell from his lips and he spoke from the fervor of his heart for he had been chosen by God to be simple and unlearned, using none of the erudite words of human wisdom; and in all things he bore himself with simplicity. Many people mocked him as a madman, but others were moved to tears when they saw how quickly he had passed from worldly pampering and vanity to loving God. He paid no heed to ridicule and gave thanks to God in great fervor of spirit.
>
> It would be difficult to specify all the hard work that had to be done to restore the church. At home Francis had been coddled, whereas now he carried a load of stones on his own shoulders and endured many hardships for love of God.
>
> *Legend of the Three Companions, 21.*

Oil for the sanctuary lamp

Francis wanted a lamp to be kept burning in front of the crucifix that had given him the order that began to make sense of his life. However, he needed oil and the poor priest couldn't buy it. So, once again, Francis set off for Assisi to beg:

> In the meanwhile he was working steadily at restoring the church,

and, because he wished that the light should be kept burning, he went through the city begging for oil. On approaching one house he saw a number of men busy playing and gambling; and overcome by shyness he turned away being ashamed to go in and beg from them. But then he thought better of it, and accusing himself of sin, he hurried back to the place, went in, and confessed his fault to all the company, how he had been ashamed to ask them for alms. He entered the house in fervor of spirit for love of God, and begged in French for oil for the church of Saint Damian.

Legend of the Three Companions, 24.

Begging for food

Begging for stones and oil isn't easy when you are the son of Pietro di Bernardone; however, you can convince yourself that this isn't for me, but for God. Francis, however, knew that he had to take one further step. He could not continue depending on the good priest at San Damiano to take care of him:

The priest who watched his labors saw how fervently he gave himself to the service of God laboring even beyond his strength; and though the priest himself was a poor man, he procured special food for Francis because he knew how delicately he had been brought up, and how in his father's house he had eaten only what was excellent. Francis himself confessed that he would not touch anything he did not like.

One day, however, when he noticed that the priest was providing him with special food, he reflected: "Wherever you may happen to go, do you suppose that you will find another such priest who will treat you so kindly? This is not the life of the poor such as you wished to choose: rather you should go, bowl in hand, from door to door, and driven by hunger, collect the various morsels you may be given. It is only thus that you can live voluntarily for love of Him who was born poor, lived poor in this world, and remained naked and poor on the cross".

So, one day, with great fervor he took a bowl and went through the streets of the city begging for alms from door to door just as he had described the begging of the poor. People dropped a variety of scraps into the bowl; and knowing what his former life had been, many were exceedingly astonished at such selfdegradation and at seeing him so completely changed.

When it came to eating the contents of the bowl, Francis' stomach turned, for he had never seen such a mess, let alone tried to eat it. At last, making a great effort, he started to gulp it down, and it seemed to him the most delicious food in the world. His heart leaped with joy and he thanked God, for he realized that, though weak and afflicted in body, he was able to endure anything, however hard, for love of the Lord. He praised and thanked God who had changed what was bitter into sweetness and had comforted him in so many ways. He also asked the priest, from then onwards, not to procure or prepare any more food for him.

Legend of the Three Companions, 21-22.

Mockery and rejection

To exchange the life of a rich merchant for that of a beggar, a person would have to be crazy. At least that's what the people of Assisi thought, and they mocked him. As for Pietro di Bernardone, he cursed the son who was making his family the talk of the town. Francis was very sensitive to his father's curses and he devised a pious plan to counteract them:

When his father saw him in this pitiful plight, he was filled with sorrow, for he had loved him dearly; he was both grieved and ashamed to see his son half dead from penance and hardships, and whenever they met, he cursed Francis. When the servant of God heard his father's curses, he took as his father a poor and despised outcast and said to him: "Come with me and I will give you the alms I receive; and when I hear my father cursing me, I shall turn to you saying: "Bless me, Father"; and then you will sign me with the cross and bless me in his place". And when this happened, the beggar did indeed bless him; and Francis turned to his father, saying: "Do you not realize that God can give me a father whose blessing will counter your curses?" Many people, seeing his patience in suffering scorn, were amazed and upheld him admiringly.

One winter's day, miserably clothed, Francis was praying when his own brother passed by and said ironically to a companion: "Ask Francis to sell you a few cents worth of sweat". The servant of God heard the words and replied gaily in French: "I will sell my sweat at a higher price to my God".

Legend of the Three Companions, 23.

A greeting of peace

Admiration began to replace mockery and finally the streets of Assisi began to echo with Francis' greeting, "May the Lord give you peace!" Assisi's motto is **"Pax et bonum!"** – Peace and Goodness!, and that's the message it should convey to you.

> In later years Francis declared that it was our Lord who taught him to greet people with the words: "The Lord give you peace!" Therefore, when beginning to preach, he always gave this greeting of peace to all present. It was certainly remarkable, if not miraculous, that, before Francis' conversion these same words had been proclaimed in Assisi by a forerunner, who often greeted the folk he met in the streets with "Pax et Bonum", – Peace and All Good! This man vanished after Francis had been converted; and one may suppose that, as John the Baptist heralded Christ, so this stranger did for Francis. He indeed was filled with the spirit of prophecy; and taking up the words of his predecessor, by his own preaching and salutary counsels he was able to unite in peace many who had formerly hated each other and were living in sin.
>
> *Legend of the Three Companions, 26.*

To see the streets of Assisi

Strolling the streets of Assisi in search of St. Francis you will find houses, palazzos, chapels and churches. Some of these merit a glance; others, if time permits, you should visit.

Included are several notes on the more noteworthy spots. In each set, we are supposing that the visitor is travelling on foot from the periphery of Assisi and heading toward the **Piazza del Comune.**

1° From the basilica of San Francesco

Via S. Francesco. – N. 14 & 14 A, (left-hand side) is **the house of the "Maestri Comacini"**; the lintel bears the emblem of this group of master-masons from Lombardy. Next to the house is the picturesque **Vicolo Sant'Andrea**. At N. 12 we find the **Palazzo Giacobetti**, where the Biblioteca Communale di Assisi is located. N. 11, the Oratorio dei Pellegrini, has several interesting frescoes. N. 3, the **Monte Frumentario**, was established as a hospital in 1267; the Barberini changed it into a credit bank. Today it is an art gallery; its portico is noteworthy. Next to the **Monte Frumentario** is the **Fonte Oliveira**, a beautiful fountain which dates back to 1570. **Via Arnoldo Fortini (Via del Seminario)**. – After passing through the **Arco del Seminario** (the remains of the 13th-century city wall) the name of the street changes. N. 7, is the diocesan seminary, parts of which date back to the 13th and 14th centuries.

Via Portico. – The street name changes again; it now takes its name from the ancient portico situated in the Roman Forum. You can see its remains under the Piazza del Comune. N. 2, is the entrance to the crypt of **San Nicolo** and the Roman Forum.

2° From the Porta San Francesco

Via Fontebella. – N. 23, there is a fresco from the school of Lorenzetti. Further along, on the left, you can see the interior of the Monte Frumentario through the **Vicolo degli Esposti**. Immediately after that is the **Fonte Marcella**, a beautiful 16th century fountain. N. 12-12 D are the rear of the Monte Frumentario.

Piazzetta Garibaldi. – The street widens into a small piazza where, at the foot of **Via Cristofani**, you can find the oratory of San Lorenzo, also called **San Francescuccio**. The headquarters of the fraternity of the "Stigmata" has some frescoes on the exterior.

Via Eugenio Brizzi. – Beginning its ascent to the Piazza del Comune, the street name changes. On the right is the **Piazza Giuseppe Sbaraglini**, which leads to **Via Bernardo di Quintavalle.**

Via Giotto. – The climb becomes steeper and the street name changes again. It joins **Via Portico** and ends in the **Piazza del Comune.**

3° From Porta San Giacomo

Via S. Giacomo. – On the right is the entrance to the picturesque **Vicolo Sant'Andrea** (on the right at the top of the Vicolo a passage leads to the church of Santa Margherita; there is a beautiful view from there).

Via Metastasio. – The street name changes; N. 18 is **San Giacomo del Murorupto**, a tiny 11th century church. Further, on the right, there is a scenic view of the Umbrian plain.

Via San Paolo. – After having formed the **Piazzetta Aluigi**, the name changes again. On the right a stairway descends to **Santo Stefano**. N. 5 is the tiny 13th-century Church of **San Paolo**.

4° From the Porta San Pietro

On left, **Via del Fosso Cupo** rejoins the **Piazzetta Garibaldi** (see above).

Via Borgo San Pietro. – On the right, the Church of **San Pietro**. N. 3 is the monastery of the French Colettine Poor Clares. Opposite it is a part of the **Citadella Christiana.** On the left, **Via Francesco Pinnachi** and, on the right the passage leads toward **Porta Sementone.**

Via Sant'Apollinare. – Opposite N. 7 are the remains of the 13th-century city walls. N. 1-1 D is the **Instituto di San Giuseppe**, built from two old churches.

Via Giacomo de Martini. – N. 3-5 is the Poor Clare Monastery of San Quirico; N. 5 has a 15th-century fresco, probably by Matteo da Gualdo. On the left, **Via Giacomo de Martino** rejoins **Via Cristofani**; on the right it ends in the **Piazza del Vescovado.**

Piazza del Vescovado. – Outside the Bishop's palace is the Church of **Santa Maria Maggiore**, which has several interesting facades. From there, take the **Vicolo Buscatti** (above and to the left on the Piazza) then the **Vicolo della Volta Pinta** to the **Piazza del Comune**; or, by way of **Via Sant'Agnese** (on the right at the center of the piazza) go to **Santa Chiara.**

5° From Porta Nuova

Via Borgo Aretino. – There is nothing significant here except the view toward **Santa Chiara** and of the Umbrian plain. At the extreme end of the street is the **Porta Santa Chiara**, the remains of the 14th-century city wall.

Piazza Santa Chiara. – Here there is a parting of the ways; **Via Sant'Agnese** leads to the **Bishop's Palace**. The upper street begins with the **Arco dei Pucci**, a vestige of the 13th-century wall.

Corso Mazzini. – This street is also called **Via Ceppo della Catena** because at night it was closed to traffic by a chain. On the right is the picturesque **Vicolo Oscuro**. Further on, also on the right is **Vicolo dei Nepis**; directly opposite is the **Scaletto dello Spirito Santo** which leads to **San Francesco Piccolo.**

6° From the Porta Perlici (see p. 28)

Via Porta Perlici. – On the left is the **Via del Comune Vecchio**, with several ancient houses (Nos. 21-23); at N. 6 the courtyard of the ancient **Palazzo del Comune.** Further, on the right is the **Vicolo San Lorenzo** which leads to the tiny church of **San Lorenzo.** On the exterior of the Church is a little shrine (hardly visible) with a fresco by Colas Petruccioli. N. 1 is an old house from the 13th-century.

Piazza San Rufino. – To the left, **Via del Turrione** where, on the right, above the transept of **San Rufino** you can see some remains of the Roman theatre. On the right is **Via Santa Maria delle Rose**; N. 2 C is the **Palazzo dei Consoli** (prior to 1225). Further along is the old church of **Santa Maria delle Rose**, now a parish hall.

Via San Rufino. – On the left is the picturesque **Via Pozzo della Mensa.** On both sides there are old houses.

Piazza del Comune

Of all the buildings on the piazza, only the facade of the **Minerva** would have been familiar to Francis (in his day there

113

were even small buildings between the columns). In spite of that, the general atmosphere is hardly changed, and it is atmosphere that we are interested in.

On the extreme western end of the piazza is the Post Office, built on the foundations of the ancient church of **San Nicolo** (see p. 91). In the 15th-century a marble pulpit was erected there. St. Bernardine of Siena preached from it in 1425. On the wall there is a delicate fresco by a disciple of Simone Martini.

On the Northern side of the piazza, to the left, is **Via San Paolo.** To the right of it is the **Palazzo del Podesta**; begun in 1212, it was not finished until 1282. Next to it is the **Torre del Comune**, begun in 1275 and finished in 1305. Notice on the base of the tower the stone with the measurements on it. Next to it is the temple of **Minerva** with its six Corinthian columns; in 1539 it was transformed into a church. Further to the east is the entrance to the picturesque **Via Tiberio d'Assisi.**

On the eastern end, the piazza is ornamented with a beautiful fountain; several streets end there.

The southern extremity is almost entirely occupied by the **Palazzo dei Priori**, built in 1337. It contains the Art Gallery (Pinacotecca). Even thought it has nothing to do with St. Francis (not even with religion) you really should stop to take a look at the grotesque figures ornamenting the covered passage, the **Volta Pinta.**

VESCOVADO

Although nothing of the 13th-century bishop's residence remains, its location is nevertheless the same. Here we have the opportunity to reflect on several incidents in the life of Francis.

Francis renounces his inheritance

Ridiculed by the townspeople of Assisi because of his penitential life, Francis was imprisoned by his father. But while his father was away, his mother set him free (see p. 25):

In the meanwhile Peter Bernardone returned home; and, on finding his son gone, he added sin to sin by abusing his wife. He then went to the palace of the commune and denounced Francis to the civil authorities, demanding the restitution of the money of which he said he had been robbed by his son.

When the authorities saw how enraged Peter was, they sent a messenger to summon Francis. But he answered that, since by divine grace he had obtained freedom, he was the servant only of God and therefore no longer owed obedience to the civil authorities but was outside their jurisdiction. The city counsellor did not wish to force the issue, and answered Peter that as Francis had entered the service of almighty God he was no longer their subject.

Peter then realized that no satisfaction was to be had from the civil authorities, so he repeated his accusation before the Bishop of Assisi. The Bishop, a wise and prudent man, sent word to Francis that he must appear and answer his father's indictment; and he replied to the messenger: "I will willingly appear before the Lord Bishop who is the father and lord of souls".

He, therefore, went to the bishop who received him gladly saying: "Your father is highly incensed and greatly scandalized by your conduct. If therefore you wish to serve God, you must first of all return him his money, which indeed may have been dishonestly acquired. God would not wish you to use it for restoring the church through sin on the part of your father, whose anger will abate when he gets the money back. Trust in the Lord, my son, and act manfully, fearing nothing, for he will help you and provide you with all that is necessary for repairing the church".

Thereupon the servant of God rose joyfully, comforted by the Bishop's words and holding out the money, he said: "My Lord Bishop, not only will I gladly give back the money which is my father's, but also my clothes". Going into the bishop's room he stripped himself of his garments and placing the money on them he stood naked before the eyes of the bishop, his father, and all present and said: "Listen all of you and mark my words. Hitherto I have called Peter Bernardone my father; but because I am resolved to serve God I return to him the money on account of which he was so perturbed, and also the clothes

I wore which are his; and from now on I will say 'Our Father who art in heaven', and not Father Peter Bernardone".

Legend of the Three Companions, 18-20.

In the bishop's residence itself, there is a room (*sala della rinuncia*) to the left of the entrance which commemorates this event.

To be Catholic

One of the most characteristic traits of Franciscan spirituality is to be Catholic, always following the Church. And, for Francis, the Bishop was a symbol of that Church, and he always wanted to be under the direction of a bishop:

> All the brothers must be Catholics, [and] live and speak in a Catholic manner. But if any of them has strayed from the Catholic faith and life, in word or in deed, and has not amended his ways, he should be completely expelled from our fraternity. And we should regard all clerics and all religious as our lord in those things which pertain to the salvation of the soul and who have not deviated from our religion, and, in the Lord, we should respect their order and their office and government.

The Earlier Rule, Chapter 19.

Counsellor and friend

Guido, Bishop of Assisi, was Francis' friend, counsellor and protector. We can reflect on some of the conversations between these two. For example, Francis tells Guido one of the reasons he wants to have no possessions:

> The brothers often asked the advice of the bishop, who received Francis with kindness, but said: "It seems to me that it is very hard and difficult to possess nothing in the world". To this blessed Francis replied: "My Lord, if we had any possessions we should also be forced to have arms to protect them, since possessions are a cause of dis-

putes and strife, and in many ways we should be hindered from loving God and our neighbor. Therefore in this life we wish to have no temporal possessions".

The bishop was greatly pleased by these words of God's servant; and indeed Francis despised all passing things, especially money, so much that he laid the greatest stress on holy poverty and insisted that the brothers should be most careful to avoid money. He made and tried several rules before the last one which he left to his brothers; and in one of these he expressed the scorn in which money should be held: "Let us beware that, having left all things, we do not forfeit eternal life for so worthless and mean a thing; and if somewhere we should happen to find money, let us treat it as the dust under our feet".

Legend of the Three Companions, 35.

Sister Death

In the bishop's palace Francis spent the last months of his life (1226), preparing to welcome our Sister Death:

At the time when blessed Francis returned from the friary of Bagnara, he was very sick and confined to bed in the episcopal palace of Assisi. The inhabitants feared that he might die during the night without their knowledge and that the brothers would secretly take his body away and bury it in another city. So they decided to keep a sharp lookout every night near the palace. At that time blessed Francis was very weak. To comfort his soul and ward off discouragement in the midst of his grave and serious infirmities, he often had the brothers sing for him the "Praises of the Lord" which he had previously composed during his sickness. He also had the Praises sung at night for the edification of those who were on guard because of him near the palace.

Brother Elias, seeing that in this way blessed Francis derived joy and courage in the Lord in the midst of such great suffering, said to him one day: "My dearest brother, I am very consoled and edified to see the joy that you experience and manifest to your companions in such affliction and sickness. Surely the men of this city venerate you as a saint in life and in death; but since they firmly believe that your serious and incurable sickness will soon lead to your death, they could think and say to themselves as they hear the "Praises of the Lord" sung: How can he display such great joy when he is going to die? Would it not be better to think of death?"

Blessed Francis answered him: "Do you remember the vision at Foligno where you told me a voice warned you that I would not live beyond two years? Before you had your vision, thanks to the Holy Spirit who puts every good thought in the heart and every good word on the lips of his faithful, I often thought of death, day and night. Since your vision. I have been, even more zealous in thinking of the hour of my death every day". Then he added with emotion: "Brother, let me rejoice in the Lord and sing his praises in the midst of my infirmities: by the grace of the Holy Spirit I am so closely united to my Lord, that, through his goodness, I can indeed rejoice in the Most High himself".

In those days a doctor from Arezzo, named Buongiovanni (Good John), a friend and favorite of blessed Francis, came to the palace to see him. The saint questioned the doctor about his sickness and said to him: "What do you think, Brother John, of my dropsy?" (Blessed Francis did not want to call those whose name was "Good" by their name out of respect for the Lord who said: "No one is good but God alone". Likewise in his letters he called no one *father or master* out of respect for the Lord who said: "You must call no one on earth your father, ... nor must you allow yourselves to be called teachers").

The doctor answered him: "Brother, with the grace of God, all will be well". He did not want to tell him that he was going to die soon. Blessed Francis replied: "Brother, tell me the truth, what is your prognosis? Do not be afraid; for, thanks to God, I am not a coward who fears death. The Lord, by his grace and in his goodness, has so closely united me to himself that I am as happy to live as I am to die". The doctor answered him: "Father, according to our medical science, your disease is incurable, and you will die either at the end of September or the fourth day of the nones of October". Then blessed Francis who was lying on his bed in an extremely weakened condition, extended his arms and raised his hands toward the Lord with great devotion and respect, crying out, his body and soul permeated with joy: "Welcome, Sister Death!"

Legend of Perugia, 64-65.

Praised be You, my Lord, through our Sister Bodily Death,
from whom no living man can escape.
Woe to those who die in mortal sin.
Blessed are those whom death will find in Your most holy will,
for the second death shall do them no harm.
Praise and bless my Lord and give Him thanks and serve Him with great humility.

Cancicle of the Creatures.

Outside Assisi

For those who can stay in Assisi longer, here are a few brief descriptions of some places that merit a visit, some for their Franciscan interest, others for touristic reasons.

The Abbey of San Benedetto

To find the abbey, leave Assisi by the Porta Nuova and, after 500 meters, go left on Via Madonna dell'Ulivo; (after about 2 km. there is a small road that leads to the Monastery of Sant'Angelo de Panzo – see p. 58); take the road that goes below the Carceri. Both of these roads are accessible to cars, but drive carefully. Only two crypts of the abbey itself remain; the newer one is from the 11th century and has some beautiful romanesque capitals.

The scenic route along Subasio

A fantastic road begins near the Carceri and ends about 5 km. from Spello at Collepino; it goes along the ridge of Subasio, passing just below the summit (1,291 m.). It affords a remarkable view of the valley.

For a nice tour, go to Spello, Collepino and then, taking the route along Subasio, visit the Carceri; then take the upper road to the Abbey of San Benedetto and return to Assisi by the lower road.

Gubbio (80 km. round trip)

About 40 km. from Assisi, this beautiful city has kept its mediaeval charm as well as some of the most beautiful monuments. It was to Gubbio that Francis headed after his "stripping before the bishop" (see p. 113). On the way one should notice the road which leads to the Abbey of San Verecondo (today Vallingegno) where Francis was treated as a poor man. The church of San Francesco incorporates the remains of the house of his friend Spadalunga, who gave him a tunic.

> At length, coming to a certain cloister of monks, he spent several days there as a scullion, wearing a ragged shirt and being satisfied to be filled only with broth. But, when all pity was withdrawn from him and he could not get even an old garment, he left the place, not moved by anger, bur forced by necessity; and he went to the city of Gubbio, where he obtained a small tunic from a certain man who once had been his friend. Then, after some time had elapsed, when the fame of the man of God was beginning to grow and his name was spread abroad among the people, the prior of the aforementioned monastery recalled and realised how the man of God had been treated and he came to him and begged pardon for himself and for his monks out of reverence for the Savior.
>
> *1 Celano, 16.*

Cannara, Bevagna, Montefalco, Foligno (60 km. round trip)

From Assisi, take the road toward Foligno; after the sign *"Passaggio d'Assisi"*, a small road on the right leads to **Cannara.** Leave the city by the Porta dei Molini and take the old road to Bevagna. On that route, between two brooks, the Fosso Rapace and the Fosso Fossato, there is the **Pian d'Arca** where, local tradition says, Francis preached to the birds.

> Meanwhile, while many were joining the brothers, as was said, the most blessed father Francis was making a trip through the Spoleto valley. He came to a certain place near Bevagna where a very great number of birds of various kinds had congregated, namely, doves, crows, and some others popularly called daws. When the most blessed servant of God, Francis, saw them, being a man of very great fervor and great tenderness toward lower and irrational creatures, he left his compan-ions in the road and ran eagerly toward the birds. When he was close enough to them, seeing that they were waiting expectantly for him, he greeted them in his usual way. But, not a little surprised that the birds did not rise in flight, as they usually do, he was filled with great joy and humbly begged them to listen to the word of God. Among the many things he spoke to them were these words that he added: "My brothers, birds, you should praise your Creator very much

and always love him; he gave you feathers to clothe you, wings so that you can fly, and whatever else was necessary for you. God made you noble among his creatures, and he gave you a home in the purity of the air; though you neither sow nor reap, he nevertheless protects and governs you without any solicitude on your part. At these words, as Francis himself used to say and those too who were with him, the birds, rejoicing in a wonderful way according to their nature, began to stretch their necks, extend their wings, open their mouths and gaze at him. And Francis, *passing through their midst, went on his way* and returned, touching their heads and bodies with his tunic. Finally he blessed them, and then, after he had made the sign of the cross over them, he gave them permission to fly away to some other place. But the blessed father went his way with his companions, rejoicing and giving thanks to God, whom all creatures venerate with humble acknowledgement. But now that he had become simple by grace, not by nature, he began to blame himself for negligence in not having preached to the birds before, seeing that they had listened to the word of God with such great reverence. And so it happened that, from that day on, he solicitously admonished all birds, all animals and reptiles, and even creatures that have no feeling, to praise and love their Creator, for daily, when the name of the Savior had been invoked, he saw their obedience by personal experience.

1 Celano, 58.
See also *Fioretti, 16.*

Bevagna is an ancient Roman city which Francis must have passed through several times. Notice the buildings in the main piazza, especially the church of St. Michael.

From there, continue on to **Montefalco** to visit at least the old church of **San Francesco**, now a museum. It contains many interesting frescoes, especially the cycle of Benozzo Gozzoli (1452) dedicated to St. Francis. These frescoes, which have never been restored, have retained their original clarity.

Trevi, Bovara, Spoleto, Monteluco (115 km. round trip)

Take the road toward Foligno then to Spoleto. About 8 km. from Foligno, on the right, is a road lading to **Pietrarossa.** Here there was a leprosarium which Francis must have visited; there is now a lovely little church decorated with frescoes. Returning to the road to Spoleto, on the left you see the picturesque town of **Trevi** on the knoll.

Further, on the left, a road leads to **Bovara** where Brother Pacifico's vision occurred. The church of St. Peter, now a theater, still maintains its primitive aspect. Next to it is a charming cloister.

One day blessed Francis was going through the valley of Spoleto; he was accompanied by Brother Pacificus, a native of the March of Ancona, who formerly in the world had been dubbed "the king of poets". Pacificus was a master of noble and courtly song. They were given hospitality in the leprosarium of Trevi. Blessed Francis said to Brother Pacificus: "Let us go to Cannara, to the church of St. Peter for I want to spend the night there". This church, situated not far from the leprosarium, had no resident priest for at that time Trevi was in ruins and had only a few inhabitants.

On the way, Francis said to Brother Pacificus: "Go back to the leprosarium: I want to be alone tonight; return tomorrow before daylight". When he was alone, Francis recited Compline and other prayers, and then wanted to rest and sleep. But he could not, for his mind was beset with fear and disturbed by suggestions from the Devil. He got up immediately, went outside of the church and made the sign of the cross, saying: "Devils! I command you on behalf of God almighty, use all the power given you by the Lord Jesus Christ to make my body suffer. I am ready to endure everything, for I have no greater enemy than my body; in this way you will avenge me on this adversary and enemy". The suggestions ceased immediately. Returning to the place where he wanted to spend the night, he fell asleep and rested peacefully.

In the morning Brother Pacificus joined him. Blessed Francis was standing before the altar inside the choir, praying. Pacificus waited for him outside the sanctuary before the crucifix, praying to the Lord. Hardly had he begun his prayer when he was caught up in ecstasy, whether in the body or outside it, God alone knows. He saw a host of thrones in the sky; one, higher than all the others, was radiant with the glory and brilliance of all kinds of precious stones. Admiring its splendor, he wondered what this throne was and for whom it was prepared. Suddenly he heard a voice say to him: "This was Lucifer's throne. Blessed Francis will occupy it in his stead".

When Pacificus had regained his senses, Francis left the choir and approached him. The brother immediately threw himself at the feet of blessed Francis, his arms in the form of a cross; for, in view of his vision, he already considered him as an inhabitant of heaven. He said to him: "Father, forgive me my sins and pray the Lord to pardon me and have pity on me. " Blessed Francis extended his hand, raised him up and saw that he had seen a vision during his prayer; he seemed to be completely transformed but as one of the elect already reigning in heaven. Pretending that nothing had happened, for he did not want to reveal his vision, he asked blessed Francis: "Brother, what do you think of yourself?" "I think", he answered, "that I am the greatest of sinners". Immediately Brother Pacificus heard the voice in his heart saying to him: "By this sign you will recognize the truth of your vision: just as Lucifer was hurled from his throne because of his pride, so will blessed Francis deserve to be exalted because of his humility and take his place".

Legend of Perugia, 23.

Continuing toward Spoleto, we find the source of the Clitumno.

At **Spoleto**, before his conversion, Francis had a dream which upset all of his plans:

Now it happened that, after the start for Apulia, Francis, felt unwell on arriving at Spoleto; and thinking with apprehension about the journey, he went to bed; but, half asleep, he heard a voice calling and asking him whither he was bound. He replied, telling of his plan. Then he, who had previously appeared to him in sleep, spoke these words:

"Who do you think can best reward you, the Master or the servant?"

"The Master", answered Francis.

"Then why do you leave the Master for the servant, the rich Lord for the poor man?"

Francis replied: "O Lord, what do you wish me to do?"

"Return to your own place", he was bidden, "and you will be told what to do. You must interpret your vision in a different sense. The arms and palace you saw are intended for other knights than those you had in mind; and your principality too will be of another order".

Francis awoke and began to turn all this over in his mind. After the first vision he had been in a transport of delight, filled with desires for worldly prosperity; but this one left him puzzled and perplexed. He thought about it so intensely that he slept no more that night. Immediately at daybreak he started back towards Assisi in glad expectation that God, who had shown him the vision, would soon reveal his will for the future. Francis now waited to be guided by him for the salvation of his soul. His mind was changed and he gave up all thought of going to Apulia.

Legend of the Three Companions, 6.

At Spoleto you should at least visit the cathedral where the letter which Francis himself wrote to Brother Leo is preserved. Not far from it is the little Romanesque church of St. Euphemia.

Leave Spoleto and head south toward **Monteluco**. At the bottom of the road is the church of San Pietro; about half-way up the hill are the remains of the Abbey of S. Giuliano and an overlook from which there is a remarkable view of the whole Umbrian valley.

It is there that, in 1218, Francis obtained from the Benedictines the little chapel in Monteluco where he constructed a small hermitage where he probably stayed several times, although his biographers do not mention it. The convent itself dates from the time of the Observant reform.

Rieti Valley (350 km. round trip)

In order to grasp the spirit of St. Francis a visit to the Rieti Valley and its hermitages is a necessary complement to your visit to Assisi. It would be best to devote enough time to this visit; however, you could manage it in a long one-day excursion from Assisi.

Take the road toward Foligno, then toward Spoleto and head towards Terni. About 17 Km. from Spoleto take the road to the left (sign indicates Rieti) which passes by Montefranco and Arrone to join the Terni-Rieti road near Piediluco. Head toward Rieti. After 115 km. take a left turn towarrd **Poggio-Bustone**, pass the village and head toward the convent of San Giacomo. Francis came here for the first time in 1208. Here, according to tradition, he was assured that his sins would be forgiven.

> Therefore the blessed father Francis was being daily filled with the consolation and the grace of the Holy Spirit; and with all vigilance and

solicitude he was forming his new sons with new learning, teaching them to walk with undeviating steps the way of holy poverty and blessed simplicity. One day, when he was wondering over the mercy of the Lord with regard to the gifts bestowed upon him, he wished that the course of his own life and that of his brothers might be shown him by the Lord; he sought out a place of prayer, as he had done so often, and he persevered there for a long time *with fear and trembling standing before the Lord of the whole earth*, and he thought in *the bitterness of his soul* of the years he had spent wretchedly, frequently repeating this word: *O God, be merciful to me the sinner*. Little by little a certain unspeakable joy and very great sweetness began to flood his innermost heart. He began also to stand aloof from himself, and, as his feelings were checked and the darkness that had gathered in his heart because of his fear of sin dispelled, there was poured into him a certainty that all his sins had been forgiven and a confidence of his restoration to grace was given him. He was then caught up above himself, and absorbed in a certain light; the capacity of his mind was enlarged and he could see clearly what was to come to pass. When this sweetness finally passed, along with the light, renewed in spirit, he seemed changed into another man.

And them, coming back, he said with joy to his brothers: "*Be strengthened*, dear brothers, *and rejoice in the Lord*, and do not be sad because you seem so few; and do not let either my simplicity or your own dismay you, for, as it has been shown me in truth by the Lord, God will make us grow into a very great multitude and will make us increase to the ends of the world. For your profit I am compelled to tell you what I have seen, though I would much rather remain silent, were it not that charity urges me to tell you. I saw a great multitude of men coming to us and wanting to live with us in the habit of our way of life and under the rule of our blessed religion. And behold, the sound of them is in my ears as they go and come according to the command of holy obedience. I have seen, as it were, the roads filled with their great numbers coming together in these parts from almost every nation. Frenchmen are coming. Spaniards are hastening, Germans and Englishmen are running, and a very great multitude of others speaking various tongues are hurrying".

1 Celano, 26-27.

It was also here that, in concern for the truth, during a sermon Francis confessed that he had eaten vegetables prepared with lard (2 Celano, 131).

Descending from Poggio-Bustone, head to Rieti. That city is

filled with memories of Francis because he stayed there several times, especially in 1225 when he was having his eyes treated. It was there one night that he heard the zither played by the angel.

At the time when blessed Francis was living at Rieti, he occupied a room in the house of Teobaldo Saraceni for a few days: he was undergoing treatment for his eyes there. One day he said to one of his companions who had learned to play the zither when he was in the world: "Brother, *the children of this world* have no understanding of the things of God. Formerly, the saints used such musical instruments as the zither, psalteries, and others to praise God and console their soul; now these instruments promote vanity and sin, contrary to the will of the Lord. I wish you would secretly procure a zither from a respectable man and play me some beautiful music; afterwards, we will put words and the "Praises of the Lord" to it. My body is afflicted with marly severe pains; I would like in this way to change the physical suffering into joy and spiritual consolation". It should be said that during his sickness blessed Francis had composed the "Praises of the Lord". Sometimes he had the brothers sing them for the glory of God, the consolation of his soul, and the edification of their neighbors. The brother answered him: "Father, I would he ashamed to go and procure that instrument for myself: the people of this city know that when I was a layman, I learned how to play the zither, and I fear that they will fancy that I am tempted to play it again". "In that case", said the saint, "Let's not talk about it any more".

The next night, around midnight, unable to sleep, he heard a zither near the house where he was staying. Its song was the most exquisite and the sweetest that he had ever heard in his life. The musician withdrew but could still be heard. Then, he returned and played without interruption for a good hour. Blessed Francis, considering that the hand of God and not the hand of man was at work in this, was filled with utmost joy. In the joy of his heart he fervently praised the Lord who had condescended to grant him so great and so rare a consolation. In the morning on rising, he said to his companion: "Brother, I asked you but you did not grant my request, but the Lord who consoles his friends in their tribulations deigned this night to console me". And he told him what had happened. The brothers were in admiration, believing that this was a great miracle. They were sure that God himself had intervened for the consolation of blessed Francis, for by a decree of the podestà no one could go about in the city, not only in the middle of the night but even as early as the third ringing of the bells. Moreover, as the saint himself declared, the zither came and went in silence, without words or any vocal noise for one hour for the consolation of his soul.

Legend of Perugia, 24.

The house of Theobald Saraceni is located on Via S. Rufo near the little church of the same name.

By way of Via Ricci near the railroad station in Rieti you will find the way to the convent of **La Foresta**. Francis stayed here with the priest who served the little church. The many people who came to see Francis had ruined the poor priest's vineyards and Francis promised him at least a better-than-usual harvest:

Around the same time blessed Francis was staying near the church of St. Fabian to have his eyes attended to. This church was near the gates of this city and was in the care of a poor secular priest. As it so happened, the Lord Pope Honorius was residing at that time in this city with the cardinals. A number of the cardinals accompanied by clerics, almost daily visited the saint out of respect and devotion. The church had a small vineyard near the house where Father Francis was staying. Since this house had but one door, all those who came to see him passed through the vineyard. The grapes were ripe, and the pleasant spot tempted one to take a siesta there: the vineyard was almost completely pillaged; certain ones picked the grapes and either ate them right on the spot or took them home, while others trampled them under foot. The priest was scandalized and disturbed: "This year", he said, "my vintage is lost. The vineyard is small but every year I harvest enough grapes for my needs".

Informed of this, blessed Francis summoned the priest to him and said: "Stop being disturbed and scandalized: nothing can be done about it. Place your trust in the Lord, because through me, his poor servant, he can repair the damage. Tell me: how many loads of wine does your vineyard produce every year?" "Thirteen", the priest answered. "Cease despairing", replied blessed Francis; "don't burden anyone with your wrongs; don't trouble anyone any more with your complaints. Have confidence in the Lord and in my words: if you harvest less than twenty loads, I promise to make up the difference". The priest agreed and kept still.

Now it so happened, thanks to God's goodness, that he did not harvest less than twenty loads, according to the saint's promise. This priest was full of admiration, as were those who were informed about it; they considered the incident a great miracle due to the merits of blessed Francis. The vineyard was, as a matter of fact, pillaged; and even if it had been laden with grapes, it seemed impossible for the priest and the others to get twenty loads of wine from it. We who lived with Francis bear testimony that when he had said: "So it is", or "So it shall be", his word was always fulfilled. We have seen many of his promises fulfilled in this away, both during his life and after his death.

Legend of Perugia, 25.
see also *Fioretti, 19.*

Return to Rieti and from there head east. After 3.5 km take the road on the left toward **Fonte-Colombo**. It is here that, in 1223, Francis composed the second Rule of his Order.

When the Order was already well established and Francis was thinking of having the rule which had been approved by Pope Innocent confirmed for all time by his successor Pope Honorius, God granted him the following vision. He saw himself picking up some tiny crumbs of bread from the ground, with which he had to feed a large number of friars who were standing about. The crumbs were so small that he was afraid to distribute them lest they slip through his fingers. Then he heard a voice from heaven telling him, "Francis, make one piece out of all those crumbs and give it to those who are willing to eat it". He did so, and the friars who failed to accept it with due reverence, or despised it when they had taken it, were soon seen to be suffering from leprosy. He was upset because he could not understand the meaning of his vision; but the following day, while he was watching in prayer, he heard a voice telling him, "Francis, those crumbs, the other night, are the words of the Gospel. The single piece is the rule and the leprosy is wickedness".

And so Francis decided to shorten the rule which he wanted to have confirmed, because it had become too long by the addition of numerous texts from the Gospel, as his vision indicated. Then he was led by the Holy Spirit into the mountains with two companions, where he fasted on bread and water; and there he dictated the rule as the Holy Spirit inspired him in his prayer. When he came down from the mountain, he gave the rule to the vicar of the Order; but a few days later the vicar claimed that he had accidentally mislaid it, and so the saint went into solitude once more and rewrote the rule just as before, as if he heard the words from God's own lips. Afterwards he obtained papal confirmation for it from his holiness Pope Honorius, who was then in the eighth year of his pontificate.

Francis used to exhort the friars fervently to be faithful to the rule, saying that he had dictated everything as it was revealed to him by God and that nothing he had prescribed came from himself. This was proved by God's own testimony only a short time afterwards when Francis received the stigmata of our Lord Jesus Christ. This was the seal of Christ, the supreme High Priest, with which he gave the rule and its author his divine approval, as we shall explain later when we have finished describing Francis' virtues.

Legenda Major, IV, 11.
see also *Legend of Perugia, 113.*

It was also at Fonte-Colombo that, toward the end of his life, Francis was handed over to the doctors who treated his eyes in vain. They decided to cauterize his temples and Francis asked "Brother Fire" to be gentle with him:

When the preferable season for eye-treatment was approaching, blessed Francis left this friary although his sickness caused him much suffering. His head was covered with a large hood that the brothers had made for him. Since he could not bear daylight, he wore a woolen and linen band over his eyes sewed to his hood. His companions led him by horseback, to the hermitage of Fonte Colombo, near Rieti, to consult a physician of that city, an eye specialist. This man came to examine blessed Francis and told him that he would have to cauterize the cheek up to the eyebrow in order to relieve the most affected eye. But the saint did not want to begin the treatment before the arrival of Brother Elias. He was expected but did not arrive, because he was detained by all kinds of hindrances. The saint hesitated to let himself be treated. In the end he was obliged to give in, but he did so especially out of obedience to the lord bishop of Ostia and to the minister general. He found it bitterly repugnant to be so concerned about himself; that is why he wanted the decision to come from his minister.

One night when the pain prevented him from sleeping, he had pity and compassions on himself and said to his companions: "My dearest brothers and my little children, bear with joy the pain and fatigue that my infirmity causes you. The Lord will take the place of his poor servant to recompense you both in this world and in the next; he will credit you with the good works that you have to neglect in order to take care of me. You will obtain an even greater recompense than those who serve the whole Order. You should say to me: "We are making a loan to you, and the Lord will pay your debts to us"". The holy Father spoke in this fashion to encourage and sustain the weak and scrupulous who might have thought: "We can no longer pray, and this

129

additional fatigue is beyond our strength". He also wanted to fore-warn them against sadness and discouragement, lest they lose the merit of their fatigues.

One day the doctor arrived with his cautery to treat his eyes. He had a fire lighted and put the instrument in it so that it would become red-hot. Blessed Francis, to comfort his soul and calm his anxiety, said to the fire: "Brother Fire, the Lord created you as something noble and useful among all creatures. Be courteous to me in this hour, for I have always loved you and will continue to do so for the love of the Lord who created you. I pray our common Creator to temper your heat that I may be able to endure it". After saying this prayer, he made the sign of the cross over the fire. All of us who were with him had to leave because we were overcome by emotion and pity; only the doctor remained with him.

After the operation, we returned and he said to us: "Cowards! Men of little faith! Why did you run away? In truth I say to you, I felt no pain whatsoever, not even the heat of the fire. If it is not burnt enough, then start all over again and burn it even more!" The doctor, noting that he did not even give a twitch, considered this a great miracle. He said to the brothers: "And yet he is a frail and sick man. I would hes-itate to make a similar burn on men with a robust and healthy body, for fear that they could not bear it, as I have experienced more than once". The burn was a long one; it extended from the ear to the eye-brow. For years a fluid accumulated night and day in the eyes; and that is why the doctor thought it well to treat the veins from the ear to the eyebrow. Other doctors who were opposed to this procedure con-sidered the operation inadvisable; and this proved to be correct, for it brought him no relief. Another pierced both ears to no avail.

Legend of Perugia, 46-48.

Doctor and patient had a very good rapport. One day Fran-cis wanted to serve a meal to those who were taking care of him.

At that time, blessed Francis was staying at the hermitage of the brothers of Fonte Colombo, near Rieti for treatment of his eyes. One day the eye doctor came to visit him and talked with him, as usual, for an hour: he was preparing to leave when the saint said to one of his companions: "Go and have a good meal served to our doctor". His companions answered him: "Father, we blushingly admit that our food supply is so low at this moment that we are ashamed to invite him and offer him anything to eat". Blessed Francis answered: "O men of little faith, do not make me repeat myself". The doctor said to blessed Francis and his companions: "Brother, it is precisely because the brothers are so poor that it would be a pleasure to eat with them". This doctor was very rich and, although the saint and his companions had often invited him, he never wanted to share a meal with them. The brothers went and prepared the table and blushingly placed on it the little bread and wine they had as well as a few vegetables that they had prepared for themselves. All sat down at table.

Hardly had the meal begun when someone knocked on the door of the hermitage: a brother got up to answer it: it was a woman who was bringing a large basket full of white bread, fish, lobster-pie, some honey, and some grapes that seemed to have been freshly picked. All this was sent to blessed Francis by the lady of a castle about seven miles from the hermitage. Whereupon the brothers and the doctor were in great admiration as they pondered the sanctity of the Father. The doctor said to the brothers: "My brothers, neither you nor I appreciate as we should the sanctity of this man".

Legend of Perugia, 26.

Take the road towards Terni; 12 km. farther, on the left, a small road leads to the convent of **Greccio**, nestled on the flank of the hillside. It is the memory of the Christmas celebration that attracts us to this place:

Francis' highest intention, his chief desire, his uppermost purpose was to observe the holy Gospel in all things and through all things and, with perfect vigilance, with all zeal, with all the longing of his mind and all the fervor of his heart, "to follow the teaching and the footsteps of our Lord Jesus Christ". He would recall Christ's words through persistent meditation and *bring to mind his deeds* through the most penetrating consideration. The *humility of the incarnation and the charity of the passion occupied his memory particularly*, to the extent that he wanted to think of hardly anything else. What he did on the birthday of our Lord Jesus Christ near the little town called Greccio in the third year before his glorious death should especially be noted and recalled with reverent memory. In that place there was a certain man by the name of John, of good reputation and an ever better life, whom blessed Francis loved with a special love, for in the place where he lived he held a noble and honorable position in as much as he had trampled upon the nobility of his birth and pursued nobility of soul. Blessed Francis sent for this man, as he often did, about fifteen days before the birth of the Lord, and he said to him: "If you want us to celebrate the present feast of our Lord at Greccio, go with haste and diligently prepare what I tell you. For I wish to do something that will recall to memory the little Child who was born in Bethlehem and set before our bodily eyes in some way the inconveniences of his infant needs, how he lay in a manger, how, with an ox and an ass standing by, he lay upon the hay where he had been placed". When the good and faithful man heard these things, he ran with haste and prepared in that place all the things the saint had told him.

But the day of joy drew near, the time of great rejoicing came. The brothers were called from their various places. Men and women of that neighborhood prepared with glad hearts, according to their means, candles and torches to light up that night that has lighted up all the days and years with its gleaming star. At length the saint of God came, and finding all things prepared, *he saw it and was glad*. The manger was prepared, the hay had been brought, the ox and ass were led in. There simplicity was honored, poverty was exhalted, humility was commended, and Greccio was made, as it were, a new Bethlehem.

The night was lighted up like the day, and it delighted men and beasts. The people came and were filled with new joy over the new mystery. The woods rang with the voices of the crowd and the rocks made answer to their jubilation. The brothers sang, paying their debt of praise to the Lord, and the whole night resounded with their rejoicing. The saint of God stood before the manger, uttering sighs, overcome with love, and filled with a wonderful happiness. The solemnities of the Mass were celebrated over the manger and the priest experienced a new consolation. The saint of God was clothed with the vestments of the deacon, for he was a deacon, and he sang the holy Gospel in a sonorous voice. And his voice was a strong voice, a sweet voice, a clear voice, a sonorous voice, inviting all to the highest rewards. Then he preached to the people standing about, and he spoke charming words concerning the nativity of the poor King and the little town of Bethlehem. Frequently too, when he wished to call Christ *Jesus*, he would call him simply the *Child of Bethlehem*, aglow with overflowing love for him; and speaking the word *Bethlehem*, his voice was more like the bleating of a sheep. His mouth was filled more with sweet affection than with words. Besides, when he spoke the name *Child of Bethlehem* or *Jesus*, his tongue licked his lips, as it were, relishing and savoring with pleased palate the sweetness of the words. The gifts of the Almighty were multiplied there, and a wonderful vision was seen by a certain virtuous man. For he saw a little child lying in the manger lifeless, and he saw the holy man of God go up to it and rouse the child as from a deep sleep. This vision was not unfitting, for the Child Jesus had been forgotten in the hearts of many; but, by the working of his grace, he was brought to life again through his servant St. Francis and stamped upon their fervent memory. At length the solemn night celebration was brought to a close, and each one returned to his home with holy joy.

1 Celano, 84-86.

But we should also take this opportunity to reflect on the Third Order, for a fraternity existed in Greccio already during the lifetime of St. Francis:

The brothers of the friary at Greccio were virtuous and poor, and the inhabitants of the country, despite their poverty and simplicity, were more pleasing to blessed Francis than those of the rest of the province. Consequently, he often went there to relax or tarry. There was an especially small, poor, and very solitary cell here to which holy Francis liked to withdraw. His example, his preaching, and that of his brothers were the reason, together with the grace of God, why many of the inhabitants entered the Order. Many women took the vow of virginity and adopted a religious habit; each one had her own house, but they led a common life; they practiced virtue, mortification, fasting and prayer; one got the impression that they were living apart from the world and their relatives; despite their youthful age and their great simplicity, they seemed to have been formed by holy religious women who had been in the service of Christ for a long time. That is why blessed Francis often said to the brothers, in speaking of the men and women of this town: "There is no large city where so many have been converted to penance; and still, Greccio is only a small town".

The brothers at Greccio, as was the custom of the brothers at that time in many of the friaries, sang the praises of the Lord in the evening. Then, men and women, great and small, would come out of their homes, stand on the road before the town, and alternate with the brothers, repeating in a loud voice: "Blessed be the Lord God". Even the little children who hardly knew how to talk praised God according to their ability.

Legend of Perugia, 34.

And finally here we can also see one of the oldest, and probably most authentic pictures of Francis.

Going to Terni, you should admire the **Cascata delle Mar-**

more which, unfortunately, functions only on Sundays for a limited time.

Outside of the Rieti valley, about 20 km. from Terni, one last hermitage deserves a visit, the **Speco of Sant'Urbano**. To go there, leave Terni and follow the signs toward Narni; then follow the road indicated to Stroncone and, after 1.2 km. take a right turn.

It was at this hermitage that, one day Francis, who was ill, said that he wanted some wine. As there was only water available, he miraculously caused it to be changed into wine:

> Another time when he was very ill at the hermitage of Sant'Urbano, Francis felt the need of something to give him strength and he asked for a glass of wine. They told him there was not a drop in the place they could give him, so he told them to bring some water. When it was brought, he blessed it with the sign of the cross and immediately it was changed into excellent wine. The poverty of a lonely friary had been unable to provide it, and so his sanctity procured it. At the taste of the wine, he immediately felt much better, so that it was clear that both the liquid and the one who drank it were supernaturally renewed. The changing of the water and the improvement in his health were so many indications of the extent to which he was "quit of the old self, and clothed in the new self" (cf. Col 3: 9-10).
>
> *Legenda Major V, 10.*

Monte Casale, La Verna (240 km. round trip)

It would be difficult to imagine a Franciscan pilgrimage which did not include La Verna. The road, which takes us through Umbertide, Città di Castello, Sansepolcro and Pieve San Stefano is not difficult.

Just before entering **Sansepolcro** you can take a right turn and go up to the little convent of **Monte Casale**, the scene of one of the numerous episodes which remind us of Francis' respect for churches and for anything connected with divine worship:

> This man, beloved of God, showed himself most devoted to divine worship and he left nothing pertaining to God dishonored because of

neglect. When he was at Monte Casale, in the province of Massa, he commanded his brothers to bring the holy relics from a church that had been abandoned by all to the place of the brothers in a most reverent manner. He was deeply grieved that they had been deprived of the devotion due them already for a long time. But when for some reason his sons had to go to some other place, they forgot the command of their father and neglected the merit of obedience. But one day, when the brothers wanted to celebrate Mass, they removed the cloth from the altar, as is customary, and there they found some very beautiful and fragrant bones. Quite astonished, they were looking at what they had never seen before. When the saint of God returned a little later, he diligently inquired if what he had commanded about the relics had been carried out. Humbly confessing the guilt of their neglected obedience, the brothers merited pardon along with punishment. And the saint said: "Blessed be the Lord my God, who himself carried out what you were to do".

2 Celano, 202.

It was also here that the characteristic episode of the conversion of the robbers took place:

In a hermitage of the brothers located north of Borgo San Sepolcro, robbers came periodically to ask the brothers for some bread; usually they hid in the tall forest which covers the region and sometimes they came out of it to rob travellers in the open country or on the highways. Certain brothers said: "It is wrong to give them alms, for they are robbers who inflict all sorts of evils on people". Others, seeing that they begged with humility and that necessity drove them to this, gave them alms at times, always encouraging them to be converted to penance.

Meanwhile, blessed Francis came to the hermitage. When the brothers asked him whether they should or should not give the robbers bread, he answered: "If you do what I am about to tell you, I have confidence in the Lord that you will win over their souls. Go and obtain some good bread and some good wine; bring them to the place where you know these men stay, and cry out: 'Come out, brother robbers! We are brothers and we have brought you some good bread and some good wine'. They will immediately come to you. Then, spread out a table cloth on the ground, put the bread and wine on it, and serve them with humility and good humor. During and after the meal, you will propose the words of the Lord to them. Then make this first request of them for the love of God: make them promise you not to

135

strike any man and not to harm anyone. That is only the beginning. Do not ask everything all at once; they would not listen to you. The robbers will promise you this because of the humility and the charity you have shown them. Another day, in gratitude for the good promise they have made to you, bring them in addition to bread and wine, some eggs and cheese, and serve them as you did the first time. After the meal, say to them: 'Why do you stay here all day long dying of hunger, suffering so much, doing so much evil in thought and in act? You will lose your souls if you are not converted to the Lord. It would be much better for you to serve God who will give you what you need for your bodies in this world and who in the end will save your souls'. And the Lord in his goodness will inspire them to be converted because of the humility and charity that you have shown them".

The brothers got up and did all that blessed Francis had counselled them to do. Through the mercy and grace of God, the robbers listened and fulfilled the brothers' requests one by one. Touched by their charity and affability, they even carried wood on their backs to the hermitage. By the mercy of God and thanks to the charity and goodness to which the brothers had given witness, some entered the Order, while others were converted to penance and promised while holding the hands of the brothers, never to do evil in the future but to live by the work of their hands. The brothers of the hermitage and those who heard the good news were full of admiration as they considered the holiness of blessed Francis and the quick conversion of these faithless and lawless men, as *foretold by him*.

Legend of Perugia, 90.
see also *Fioretti, 26.*

It was in 1213 that count Orlando of Chiusi gave the mountain of **La Verna** to Francis (see First Consideration of the Stigmata). Francis often stayed there and his biographies relate several episodes which occurred there (see *Legenda Major* VIII, 10; *Legend of Perugia*, 50, 90, etc.)

Franciscan literature is filled with episodes about St. Francis and la Verna. Here we will consider only two of them: the story of the peasant who accompanied him, and the stigmatization, which took place in September 1224, around the feast of the Holy Cross (September 14).

In August of 1224 Francis retired to La Verna to celebrate the lent of Saint Michael. On climbing the mountain, he miraculously provided a spring to satisfy the thirst of the peasant who was accompanying him:

> Once when the blessed Francis wanted to go to a certain hermitage that he might devote himself more freely to contemplation there, he obtained an ass from a certain poor man to ride on, because he was not a little weak. Since it was summer, the peasant, following the man of God up the mountain, became fatigued from the difficulty and the length of the trip; and before they had reached the place, he collapsed exhausted by a burning thirst. He called after the saint and begged him to have pity on him; he said he would die unless he would be refreshed by some drink. The holy man of God, who always had compassion on those who were suffering, got down without delay from the ass and, kneeling upon the ground, he stretched his hands toward heaven; and he did not let up in his prayers until he felt he had been heard. "Hurry", he said to the peasant, "and you will find living water over there, which Christ has just now mercifully brought from the rock for you to drink". O how astounding is the condescension of God which readily inclines him to help his servants! The peasant drank the water that came from the rock by the power of him who had prayed, and he drew drink from the hardest rock. There had never been a flow of water there before, and, as diligent search has proved, none could be found there afterwards. Why should we wonder that a man who is full of the Holy Spirit should show forth in himself the wonderful deeds of all the just? For, for a man who is joined with Christ by the gift of a special grace it is not something great if he does things similar to the things that have been done by other saints.
>
> *2 Celano, 46.*

On September 14 or 15 Francis received the Stigmata of the Passion. Here we will read the meditation which Thomas of Celano wrote about that miraculous event:

> Two years before Francis gave his soul back to heaven, while he was living in the hermitage which was called Alverna, after the place on which it stood, he saw *in the vision of God* a man standing above him, like a seraph with six wings, his hands extended and his feet joined together and fixed to a cross. Two of the wings were extended above his head, two were extended as if for flight, and two were wrapped around the whole body. When the blessed servant of the Most High saw these things, he was filled with the greatest wonder, but he could not understand what this vision should mean. Still, he

was filled with happiness and he rejoiced very greatly because of the kind and gracious look with which he saw himself regarded by the seraph, whose beauty was beyond estimation; but the fact that the seraph was fixed to a cross and the sharpness of his suffering filled Francis with fear. And so he arose, if I may so speak, sorrowful and joyful, and joy and grief were in him alternately. Solicitously he thought what this vision could mean, and his soul was in great anxiety to find its meaning. And while he was thus unable to come to any understanding of it and the strangeness of the vision perplexed his heart, the marks of the nails began to appear in his hands and feet, just as he had seen them a little before in the crucified man above him.

His hands and feet seemed to be pierced through the middle by nails, with the heads of the nails appearing in the inner side of the hands and on the upper sides of the feet and their pointed ends on the opposite sides. The marks in the hands were round on the inner side, but on the outer side they were elongated; and some small pieces of flesh took on the appearance of the ends of the nails, bent and driven back and rising above the rest of the flesh. In the same way the marks of the nails were impressed upon the feet and raised in a similar way above the rest of the flesh. Furthermore, his right side was as though it had been pierced by a lance and had a wound in it that frequently bled so that his tunic and trousers were very often covered with his sacred blood. Alas, how few indeed merited to see the wound in his side while this crucified servant of the crucified Lord lived! But happy was Elias who, while the saint lived, merited to see this wound; and no less happy was Rufino who touched the wound with his own hands. For when this Brother Rufino once put his hand upon the bosom of this most holy man to rub him, his hand fell down to the right side of Francis, as it can happen; and it happened to touch the precious wound. The holy man of God was not a little grieved at this touch, and pushing his hand away, he cried out to the Lord to forgive Rufino. For he made every effort to hide this wound from those outside the order, and he hid it with such great care from those close to him that even the brothers who were always at his side and his most devoted followers did not know of this wound for a long time. And though the servant and friend of the Most High saw himself adorned with so many and such great pearls, as with the most precious gems, and endowed in a wonderful manner above the glory and honor of all other men, he did not become vain in heart nor did he seek to please anyone out of thirst for vainglory; but, lest human favor should steal any of the grace given him, he strove in every way he could to hide it.

1 Celano, 94-95.
see also *Legenda Major, XIII.*

Too see La Verna

After Assisi **La Verna** is the place most intimately connected with the memory of St. Francis. The first cells were made of wood and branches; later, in the 14th and 15th centuries the first buildings began to develop individually or in small groups, giving the complex the look of a typical village nestled in the deep woods on the mountain ravines. Here we can consider the main features:

The chapel of the greeting of the birds, halfway up the mountainside along the old wooded road leading from below, not far from the place where the Saint furnished water to the man who accompanied him and accepted his reprimand.

The chapel of **St. Mary of the Angels**, wich Francis asked Count Orlando to build, was enlarged in 1260 and decorated with etchings and three frontals by della Robbia.

The chiesa maggiore dates from the 15-16th century; it has Renaissance chapels, 7 terracotta works of various dimensions by Della Robbia, and precious reliquaries including one with blood from the Saint's stigmata. The altar rail and Baroque altar are of polychrome marble; the choir stalls are of inlaind wood, and the organ is very valuable. Be sure to note the exterior open gallery on two sides with ancient inscriptions.

The **Quadrant Piazza** with its beautiful view of the mountains and valleys is named for the sundial found there.

Go down the steps to the **Sasso Spicco** (a cave where Francis used to go to pray); looking up you can see how the gallery passes by a bridge over the ravine to the chapel of the Stigmata. Remember that in Francis' day the bridge was not there, and there was only the log across the ravine.

Walk along the gallery along the side of the mountain, with a terracotta by Della Robbia at the beginning and frescos depicting the life of St. Francis on the walls. At one point you can go outside to the enclosed area with the deep ravine with a cave which sometimes served him as a bed. Following this, in sequence, we have the chapels **of the Crucifix, St. Anthony, St.**

Bonaventure, the Falcon, and the hollow (The Devil's Cave) on the rocky outcroopping.

Last of all, there is the little **church of the Stigmata** built on the small shelf where the miracle took place. It is richly decorated with etchings and inlay. The altar is adorned with a large frontal by Della Robbia.

On the side of the mountain there is the **chapel of Blessed John of la Verna** and on the peak the chapel of **la Penna** where you can admire a seemingly endless view.

Besides St. Francis, la Verna is filled with memories of his companions, especially **Brother Leo**, who helped the Saint and to whom he gave his written blessing; it was also here that, in 1259, St. **Bonaventure** wrote a letter to the Poor Clares and his famous work, **The Soul's Journey to God**; it was here that **Ubertino da Casale** wrote his famous *Arbor vitae* in 1305; **Blessed John of la Verna** lived here for many years and died here in 1332. His life is narrated in the **Fioretti** and the **Considerations on the Stigmata**.

Table of contents

Printed by
Tipolitografia Porziuncola
Santa Maria degli Angeli – Assisi (Pg)
march 1993